Change and Tradition
Cultural and Historical Perspectives

Nigeria:
Change and Tradition
in a West African State

Fourth Edition

William Neher
BUTLER UNIVERSITY

XanEdu

17177 Laurel Park Drive
Suite 233
Livonia, MI 48152
800-562-2147
www.xanedu.com

Contents

CHAPTER ONE

Introduction

Africans, like other peoples in the world, inhabit a present which emerged from a unique past and is moving toward an uncertain future. For Africans, as for all other peoples, this cultural dynamic has existed from the beginning. Tradition in Africa has always renewed itself in response to change. Yet when Western scholars, such as those in the United States and Europe, have spoken of African societies as traditional, they seemed to imply these societies were static, not subject to change, or unresponsive to its imperatives. The Nigerian novelist, Chinua Achebe, despairs of the Western view of his land and people. In his critique of Joseph Conrad's *Heart of Darkness*, Achebe charges that Conrad perpetuates a view of African as unchanging and unchanged.[1] This perspective fails to take account of the dynamic nature of African tradition. Tradition has never been static in Africa. It has, instead, responded to changing conditions in a continuing struggle to sustain both the glory of the past and the vitality of the present.

Africa today is a huge continent of over 600 million inhabitants, divided into over fifty different political units. The people can be further divided into as many as 3,000 cultural and linguistic groups. Despite such diversity, definitions of Africans by non-Africans frequently invoke physical characteristics of race as the single unifying factor of an entire continent of peoples. Supposed racial homogeneity has been overemphasized by Western observers, while the commonalities of situation and experience have been ignored. To understand these shared circumstances, physical and cultural, indigenous and externally imposed, is to begin to see a more complete and accurate view of what being African means and has meant.

Shared circumstances are given by ecology and by history. The lands of Africa tend to be harsh and difficult—receiving either too much rain (in the rain forests), or too little (in the deserts and savannas). Soils are often infertile; insects and parasites prey upon crops and herds, making food production difficult. All but two enclaves on the continent were suddenly annexed by European powers at the end of the nineteenth century and the beginning of the twentieth, meaning that nearly all Africans have had to deal in their recent pasts with the political and social problems of being colonized. Most African nations have achieved independence only recently,

1

and then not on the basis of traditional ethnic distinctions but on the basis instead of political boundaries fixed by the colonizing countries.

Nigeria, the focus of our study of African tradition and change, is one of the new nations of Africa—the most populous and potentially one of the most powerful. Like the rest of Africa, it is ethnically and culturally diverse (some estimates place the number of languages spoken in Nigeria at about 250). Within its borders is represented the "Triple Heritage" of Africa: the African, the Islamic, and the Christian. Each of these three traditions comprises not only a distinct religious ethos but also an entire cultural milieu—linguistic, political, and material. Islam and Christianity represent the outside forces that have shaped modern African cultures, in combination with traditional religions and indigenous world views. The northern half of Nigeria is largely Islamic, while in the southern half Christian and traditional beliefs dominate. Estimates suggest that about 49 percent of Nigeria's population is Muslim; about 34.5 percent are Christian; and about 18 percent follow traditional African religions.

Even the geographical configuration we now know as Nigeria reflects this triple heritage. There was no "nation" of Nigeria before 1912, when the country was created by the combination of two British colonized territories without regard to existing ethnic, political, or cultural identifications. The very name of the country was supplied by an outsider, Englishwoman Flora Shaw, who later married Frederick Lugard, the most famous colonial administrator of Nigeria. In these and other ways, Nigeria encapsulates the tensions and the problems characteristic of the continent as a whole.

This text focuses of three important ethnic groups of Nigeria—the Hausa of the North, the Yoruba of the Southwest, and the Igbo of the Southeast. Our study of these groups, the three largest in the country, will underscore the diversity, richness, and complexity of Africa and, at the same time, examine how these cultures have dealt with the changes wrought by colonialism and early modern nationalism.

As we begin, some terms and usages should be clarified. First, the term *tribe* or *tribal* does not appear often in this text because the term is of uncertain meaning and often carries negative connotations. Where classification is necessary, ethnic or linguistic markers are preferred, though even these are modern contrivances which do not always correspond well to patterns of self-identification in traditional Africa. The word *Yoruba*, for example, is of Hausa origin, and was used by the Hausa to refer to the great empire of Oyo. The Hausa themselves have been referred to by many different names in history; the Fulani, who became closely associated with the Hausa in Nigeria, call them the *Habe*. The word *Hausa*, from the Kanuri language of northeastern Nigeria, means west, indicating that the Hausa lived west of the Kanuri. The word *Igbo*, from the Kwa languages of West Africa, has been variously translated as *forest-dweller* or *community* and may once have referred to a much larger group of people speaking related languages.

What, then, does ethnic identification mean? Usually, ethnicity refers to a complex of cultural practices, including language, kinship organization, economic activities, location, types of dwellings, and religious practices. Once we have become better acquainted with the geography and history of West Africa, we shall return to our study of ethnicity by taking a closer look at community life among the Hausa, the Yoruba, and the Igbo.

Geographical Setting

Africa is the second largest continent, after Asia. It is three times larger than Europe and four times larger than the area of the United States. The coast of Africa has comparatively few gulfs or bays, however, with the result that the coastline itself appears shorter in total length than that of any other continent. Theories of tectonic plate movement suggest that the present African continent was at one time the center of a giant continent, from which the other continents have gradually drifted away. The African plate became isolated from the others, so that it has not been shaped by collisions with or passage of other plates, except in the northeastern corner where the Eurasian plate has had some effect, creating mountain ranges in the Ethiopia region.

Physical Features

The interior of the continent is marked by several shallow basins, which are drainage features associated with great river systems. Geographers over the years have remarked that a peculiarity of these rivers is that they all seem to take very indirect routes to their oceans. The Niger River of West Africa, from which Nigeria takes its name, flows first toward the Sahara Desert before taking a sudden turn to the south and thence out to the Atlantic through modern day Nigeria. Similarly, the Congo River flows north until it takes a sweeping turn to flow back south and west toward the Atlantic. The Zambezi River of southern Africa appears headed for the Kalahari Desert before taking an abrupt turn toward the Indian Ocean. Lake Chad, on the northern border of Nigeria, represents the drainage of a basin that never developed an outlet to an ocean (similar to the formation of Great Salt Lake in Utah).

As a result of these basins surrounded by ridges (escarpments), most of the rivers are broken by waterfalls and the rapids of cataracts where the rivers have cut their way through the ridges near the edges of the continent. Upriver travel into the African interior has been difficult historically because of these cataracts and falls. Still within the interior of the continent, rivers have often provided for ready movement of peoples. The Niger River, for example, in the region studied in this text, was a highway for trade and communication for several large African empires. A look at a physical map reveals the southern third of the continent is nearly surrounded by the "Great Escarpment," where the edge of the ridges reaches almost to the sea. Features such as this and the escarpments of the Great Rift Valley in East Africa have constituted barriers to human movement and communication over the years.

Climatic variations have also played a role in determining human movement and habitation on the African continent. From north to south, successive zones are increasingly arid and desert-like, next increasingly wet and tropical (in the Congo River Basin), and once again increasingly dry to desert-like, as in the Namib and Kalahari Deserts of Southern Africa. Between the arid and tropical zones lies the savanna that is characteristic of much sub-Saharan Africa. A savanna is open country with scattered trees and vegetation, similar to the dryer parts of the Great Plains in the United States. The wettest or most tropical areas are found both at the coasts of East and West Africa and in the area of eastern Congo, the huge area drained by the Congo River System.

The northern third of the continent is dominated by the Sahara Desert, part of an immense desert that stretches across the continents from Morocco to southern Pakistan and on to the Gobi Desert of Mongolia. The Namib Desert of southern Africa reflects the mirror image of the global climatic feature that brought about the Sahara of the North. The Sahara provides a natural barrier to human movement, similar to the seas that surround the southern half of the African continent. In fact, the southern edge of the Sahara is called the Sahel, an Arabic word which suggests a coast. Still, the Sahara has not been an impenetrable barrier. There were well-established caravan routes across the desert even by the time of the Roman Empire.

The Sahara is a fairly recent geological feature; we believe that what is now the desert was fairly well-watered and generally habitable as recently as around 5,000 B.C.E. (Before the Common Era). Since then, a process of desiccation has resulted in the desert's steady expansion to the north and south. The disastrous droughts in the Sahel in recent years, probably exacerbated by environmental mismanagement, forcefully brought this process to the attention of governments and people around the world.

The escarpments, deserts, and rainforests are all features that have contributed to isolation of human groups within Africa and have served to make contact with people from outside Africa somewhat difficult.

Within the boundaries of Nigeria, most of these geographical features of the continent as a whole are reproduced on a smaller scale. The north is mostly arid country, dry savanna. The Niger River cuts across the country from west to east, taking a sharp turn south when it joins with the Benue River, which flows from east to west from the eastern border of Nigeria. The country is thus divided into two halves: the northern plateaus, semi-arid savanna country, and, below the confluence of the two great rivers, a southern half that is further divided into two parts by the Niger River as it flows to its delta in Southern Nigeria. North of the confluence of the Niger and Benue Rivers is the highest plateau in Nigeria—the Jos Plateau, which was an important site for early iron-working.

To the south in Nigeria, increasing rainfall and vegetation culminate in mostly tropical conditions and dense forests at the coast. The delta of the Niger River is the dominant feature of the coast, as the creeks, inlets and mangrove swamps of that region stretch from the border with Cameroon nearly to the city of Lagos. Tropical conditions are more pronounced on the eastern side of the Niger, the region roughly associated with the Igbo people. Savanna conditions reach further to the south toward the coast on the western side, the area where the Yoruba people are dominant.

A further condition that has shaped human life in Africa, and particularly in Nigeria, has been the composition of soils for agriculture. The most prevalent soil on the continent is the mineral type associated with deserts, characterized by minimum fertility (about 28 percent of the continent is covered by such poor soils). An additional fifth of the soil of Africa is weakly developed or nearly infertile due to lack of moisture or erosion by wind. Almost as much of the soil is high in mineral, particularly iron, content (hence the typical red color of African soils), which is subject to loss of fertility due to leaching by water in areas of high rainfall, such as in the rainforest. Human use of some land has led to further deterioration; for example, in large parts of southern Nigeria, patches of so-called secondary forest are all that remain of what formerly were extensive rainforests.

These conditions of climate, vegetation, and soil types are factors contributing to the difficulties of African farmers as food producers in West Africa.

Food and Agriculture

These geographical features of West Africa resulted in a major division along the lines of food crops, a division represented in Nigeria, as well. In the open savannah of the north, grain or cereal crops could be grown. To the south, in the forest belt, people relied more on root crops, such as yams.

Grains are actually "ennobled grasses," so it is hardly surprising that as people began to cultivate plants, those living in savannah country would concentrate on the cultivation of grasses. The important cereals have been millet and sorghum in this savanna area. Wild sorghum is indigenous to the African continent, as may be wild millet, although this is less certain. The Ethiopian region of northeast Africa appears to have been an important early area for cultivation of both crops, although a West African cradle for these crops has not been ruled out. Wild rice was probably developed as a food crop in Ethiopia, as well, but did not become as widespread in West Africa as sorghum and millet. Cereal crops have been associated with the development of large-scale states in the western Savannah, perhaps because of the scale of organization required for such cultivation and the food surplus thus made possible.

Stretching through the forest belt of West Africa, from the Ivory Coast to the highlands of Cameroon east of Nigeria, runs the area of the *Yam Complex*. This Yam Complex is nearly coextensive with the distribution of peoples who speak the closely related languages of the *Kwa* language family (Yoruba and Igbo are both *Kwa* languages). Interestingly, the yam is not the central food product beyond the area of the *Kwa* speakers, even though it could have been. Historians assume that yam cultivation began with digging for wild yams and tubers, leading to the practice of gradual cultivation between 2500 and 1500 B.C.E. Other types of yams have been brought to Africa for cultivation, but Igbo traditions make it clear that the indigenous guinea yam is much more prestigious than imported types. In their New Yam Festival, only the traditional yams are used, and these are the only ones that count when designating farmers for honors or titles. These indigenous yams have been fully domesticated; wild yams may still be found in Nigeria and gathered by the very poor for food, but these yams are often toxic and must be pounded and boiled to be made edible.

Other food crops that appear to have been indigenous to Nigeria include cowpeas, a few species of groundnuts (known as peanuts in the U.S.), the oil palm, egusi, (a type of melon), fluted pumpkin, *okro* (or okra, an example of an Igbo word that has come into English), African breadfruit, Malagueta pepper, and kola nuts, which later became important in long-distance trade in West Africa.

Many important food crops have been borrowed from other continents. These borrowed crops have in many cases become extremely important in the diets and cultures of Africans. The eminent African historian, Jan Vansina, claims, "Cultivation of the banana revolutionized life in the forest."[2] The banana and plantain and cocoyam or taro root, all originated in Asia. Botanists agree that the banana reached Africa at least two thousand years ago.

Food Crops of the Forest Region

Major crops also came from the Americas, specifically maize (what Americans refer to as corn), cocoa as a major cash crop in modern times, and cassava, also known as manioc. Cassava is quite important in Nigeria today, because the flour of cassava, known as *garri*, is cheap, filling, and tasty.

Most food animals were borrowed from outside Africa, it appears. Cattle are signs of wealth and well-being throughout Africa. The first variety of cattle in West Africa appears from archaeological records to have been a short-horned, diminutive variety. These smaller cattle were later replaced by the larger variety known as *"Zebu"* cattle, which are humped with long curving horns. These cattle originated in India. In historical times, Zebu cattle were associated especially with the Fulani people who live throughout the savannah country of West Africa. Herds are not usually found in the forest belt because of lack of grazing land and cattle sickness caused by the tse-tse fly. While the cattle herders such as the Fulani provided butter, milk, and also manure for fertilizer, they also caused some tension because of trampled fields. Even today, cattle are raised primarily for the butter and other dairy goods they produce. In general, Africans do not eat the cattle, except for special occasions or out of necessity. Most of the diets of pastoralists are provided by non-animal, vegetable sources.

In modern times, many crops have been grown for sale and export rather than for consumption by local people. For example, in northern Nigeria today, one sees large fields of cotton and groundnuts for export markets. In the nineteenth century, palm oil became a major export crop from southern Nigeria. Used at first as a lubricant, palm oil is now used primarily for soap and food products. In the western regions of the Nigerian forest belt, cocoa has been developed as an important "cash crop" (the term means it is for export, rather than for subsistence consumption by the farmers themselves).

Summary

The physical features of the African continent, such as difficulties of upriver travel, lack of harbors, the barriers of desert, rainforest, and escarpments, have tended to create conditions of isolation from influences outside the continent. On the other hand, the open savannas, as in West Africa, and some of the great rivers, such as the Niger, have allowed for ease of internal travel and migration. The deserts were not impenetrable, moreover, and trade-routes crisscrossed even the great Sahara.

Nigeria exhibits many of the physical features of the rest of the continent as a whole, with arid lands and savanna in the North, the great Rivers Niger and Benue in the middle, and the rainforest regions to the South. Many food crops now important in Nigeria were imported from outside Africa, including maize, bananas, and cassava. In the colonial and modern times, there was a drift toward cultivating so-called "cash crops" for export, away from the subsistence agriculture which predominated in earlier times.

References

1. Chinua Achebe (1989). "An Image of Africa: Racism in Conrad's *Heart of Darkness*," in Achebe, C., *Hope and Impediments: Selected Essays*. New York: Doubleday.
2. Jan Vansina (1984). "Western Bantu Expansion," *Journal of African History*, 25, 141.

CHAPTER TWO

Historical Overview of West Africa

Sources for African History

In piecing together the human history of Africa, scholars must rely on a wide range of tools. For most African peoples, the written record begins only within the last few centuries. Other records exist in plenty, however, and provide the primary evidence which is translated by archaeology, linguistics, ethnobotany, and similar sciences into a narrative history of early Africa. Archaeologists study the record of human artifacts, such as remains of dwellings, tools, and weapons; linguists trace the development and diffusion of language; and we have already seen how botanists draw inferences about where and how people live by studying plant population and diffusion. Frequently, two sciences are used in combination. For example, the linguistic root used to denote a particular food or tool can reveal who ate the food or used the tool and where they lived. Archaeology provides a rough dating system for early times. While no historical survey can do justice to the complexities of linguistic and archaeological research, we shall look briefly at some results of such studies in West Africa.

Language and History in Africa

Linguistic evidence suggests that the majority of the current population of the southern two-thirds of the African continent settled there "recently," meaning within the last two thousand years or so. There were, of course, people already in these areas before this population expansion, probably scattered bands of hunter-gatherers who were absorbed or displaced by the new people, who undoubtedly were farmers.

This great population expansion, the so-called "Bantu migrations," is an important theme of early African history. For that reason, a little background on the meaning and function of a language family or subfamily should be helpful. As a linguistic term, "*Bantu*" denotes a language family, as do the terms "*Romance*" or "*Scandinavian*," when used as linguistic terms. (In some parts of Africa, particularly southern Africa, "Bantu" when applied to people is considered by some to be an insult.) Many people are familiar with the "Romance" languages, which include French, Spanish, Italian, and Romanian. These languages all grew out of Latin, the language of the Romans (hence "Romance"). After the break-up of the Roman Empire, the Latin of the Spaniards gradually became distinct from the Latin of the French or the Italians. Eventually, these dialects became mutually unintelligible and were recognized as separate languages. English, for another example, grew out of the Germanic languages, although the Norman Conquest of England brought French into the linguistic history of English. All these languages grew out of an older parent language in the still more distant past. Linguists today have designated a "family" relationship among a huge number of these languages including English, French, Russian, Persian, Greek, and Hindi. They comprise the *Indo-European* language family. Most of the other languages of the world similarly can be placed in a few large language families.

Nearly all the languages of Africa can be placed into four large language families, three of them represented in Nigeria. The four major families are:

1. *Afroasiatic*, which includes the Semitic languages of Arabic and Hebrew, as well as the languages of the Berbers of the Sahara Desert, the Amhara of Ethiopia, and the language of the ancient Egyptians, *Coptic*.

2. *Niger-Kordofanian*, or *Niger-Congo*, which includes many of the languages of West Africa and the huge sub-family of the Bantu languages.

3. *Nilo-Saharan*, which includes languages spoken by the Maasai of East Africa and by many peoples of the southern Sudan and the Sahelian region of West Africa.

4. *Khoisan*, or *Click* languages, which includes the San and Khoi of Southern Africa.

The distribution of these languages within their language families suggests probable routes and times of migrations. The close relatedness and broad dissemination of the Bantu languages suggests that the speakers of these languages expanded over and settled vast areas of the continent quickly and recently, roughly over a time from around 100 to about 1700 C.E. The Igbo of Nigeria are right at the boundary separating the *Kwa* languages of West Africa (mentioned in the first chapter in association with the Yam Complex) from the languages of the Bantu branch. Another such line marks the linguistic boundary between the *Mande* speakers, people in the savannas of the early Sudanic empires, and the *Kwa*-speakers. Regardless of widespread stories concerning migrations of West African peoples from the Middle East or other areas, linguistic evidence indicates that the peoples of

West Africa have lived in roughly the same areas for well over two thousand years.

As many as 250 languages are spoken in Nigeria. The Hausa language, spoken over a wide area of northern Nigeria, is of the Afroasiatic language family, which also includes Arabic and Hebrew, as noted above. The Nigerian people associated with the great historic empire of Kanem-Borno, the Kanuri, speak a language of the Saharan branch of the Nilo-Saharan family. The Nilo-Saharan language distribution also dips all the way down into East Africa and includes peoples such as the Maasai of Kenya and Tanzania. Most of the other peoples of Nigeria speak languages that belong to sub-divisions of the great Niger-Congo family. The *Kwa* languages, as we have seen, are found throughout the forest belt of West Africa, including in Nigeria and Yoruba and Igbo. The linguistic evidence indicates that the people speaking the West African languages were in or very near their current locations well before the beginning of the great diffusion of Bantu languages into Central, Eastern, and Southern Africa.

Archaeology and History: Iron Age in Nigeria

The success of the Bantu speakers shown by their wide distribution across the continent is thought to derive from their employment of agriculture and iron-working. The population increase associated with these innovations probably occurred before 1000, and even earlier for Iron Age peoples of West Africa (dates without B.C.E. are to be understood as belonging to the Common Era, or A.D. by the traditional dating system).

Archaeologists have dated iron-working in central Nigeria to the sixth or seventh century B.C.E. and in the *Nok* culture in northern Nigeria to 300 B.C.E. In addition to the signs of iron-working, terra cotta—or earthenware—masks were discovered in 1936 and 1944 on the Jos Plateau near the modern town of Nok. Since 1944 many more Nok terra cottas have been discovered, some of high artistic merit. The art of the Nok people appears to be of great antiquity and is thought to foreshadow the artistic traditions of the Yoruba.

The presence of early iron-working in Nigeria suggests that the knowledge of iron-smelting and smithing developed independently or reached this part of Africa by one or both of two routes: from the Nile River region (ancient Egypt) west across the savannahs, or from the ancient state of Carthage on the North African coast, coming south across the early Saharan trade routes. People who had mastered iron production had several

advantages over populations still using stone implements. Iron tools allowed for much more productive farming, and iron weapons were more effective in protecting farm land, as well as people, from predators. Iron-working thus led to a more rapid build-up of population and to a settled way of life in a society more highly organized than had been possible earlier.

The Sudanic Kingdoms of West Africa

The African past is a culturally rich one. Traditional societies, however organized, all had developed systems of community—systems of governance and of defense, labor, economics, architecture, art, religion, and kinship. The period of the great kingdoms of West Africa stretches over more than ten centuries, the earliest arising about 800 and the latest reaching their height by 1400. These kingdoms were of two primary types: (1) the earlier were the northern Sudanic kingdoms, which arose on the fringes of the Sahara Desert and grew rich and powerful through trans-Saharan trade in gold, salt, and textiles; (2) the more southerly kingdoms of the forest, some developing as terminus points for Saharan trade (as sources for gold, kola nuts, and other trade commodities), and others in response to the rise of Atlantic trade in slaves, weapons, and manufactured goods. A third type of socio-political organization of particular importance to our study is the small-scale or "stateless" society characteristic of the Igbo of southeastern Nigeria. We will begin with the story of the savanna empires of the Sudanic region.

Ghana, Mali, and Songhai

As early as the 700s, Arabic documents report a great empire to the south of the Sahara Desert deriving its prosperity and power from trans-Saharan trade in gold and salt. The *Ghana*, or ruler, of the empire which became known to history as the great state of Ghana, was the traditional head of a West African people known as the *Soninke*. As the Soninke gained control of the southern end of the trans-Saharan trade of gold for salt, they were able to extend their power over neighboring peoples. Militarily, this power was probably based on horses, acquired in trade and used for cavalry. In the open savannah country, cavalry provided for swift movement and communication conducive to a larger political organization. The land of the Soninke people lay between the sources for the salt in the Sahara Desert and the gold, coming north from hills south of the Niger River.

Ghana is now recognized as the first of a series of entities collectively known as the Sudanic Kingdoms of West Africa. The term, "*Sudan*," comes from the Arabic for "Land of the Black Peoples" and refers to the vast open land of the savannas sweeping from the coast of Senegal through the area drained by the Niger River to the region of Lake Chad and on to the area of the modern Republic of the Sudan, which obviously has retained the term in its name. These so-called Sudanic Empires exhibited certain common characteristics. For example, the kings or emperors were considered to be divine rulers, something like the Pharaohs of ancient Egypt. Historians today believe this similarity may be due to an earlier cultural affinity among peoples living in the Sahara when it was still well-watered and more suitable for habitation. As the desert advanced, people from this central culture area moved to the north and east (to the Nile Valley) and to the south, the area of the Sudanic kingdoms.

Two more great empires, Mali and Songhai, successively replaced early Ghana as the powers controlling the gold and salt trade of the western Sudan. There was a long break between the fall of Ghana and the rise of Mali. For a time, no single ethnic group succeeded in gaining control of the trade network. In 1230, however, a great leader of the *Mandinke* peoples appeared: *Sundiata Keita*.

Sundiata, who based his power on the creation of what we would call a standing army, established control over the gold-producing regions as well as the area of the great bend of the Niger River, taking the title of *Mansa*, or lord. In the Mandinke language, a *mansa* was any sort of chief or "owner of the land." After Sundiata, the title was used exclusively for the emperor. His great rival, whom he defeated in a climactic battle, was identified as both a blacksmith and a "magician," which probably means that Sundiata's success marked the victory of Islam over rulers who based their authority on more traditional belief systems.

His military sovereignty assured, Sundiata turned his attention to domestic matters—to caravan trade and the cultivation of crops and grains, including cotton. Thus did the Empire of Mali grow rich and Sundiata's fame grew. His story, first set down in an ancient Arabic manuscript, lives on in the stories and dances of West Africa. The *Epic of Sundiata* is still recited today, with musicians, by bards from the region of western Mali and the Gambia River.

Sundiata appears to have been only a nominal Muslim, remaining a hero of traditional religion as well as representing the coming of Islam. In the epic associated with his name, his ancestry is traced on one side from a companion of the Prophet Muhammed, and on the other, from a sorceress who could transform herself into a wild buffalo. His successors, however, were more thoroughly Muslim. The most powerful of these was *Mansa Musa*, whose spectacular pilgrimage to Mecca in 1324 included an entourage of 8,000 people in a year-long journey of some 9,000 miles. Working from the accounts of Muslim scribes, one historian writes:

> Certainly the emperor's trip was the sensation of the Moslem world. It literally put Mali on the map. Maps of Africa after this time almost always show Mali and many have drawings of Mansa Musa. They usually show him as a black emperor with robe, crown, scepter and orb of gold. Mali became fixed in people's minds as the Eldorado—country with limitless gold, and as a result, there was an even greater flow of traders, merchants, religious leaders and scholars to the empire.[1]

Mansa Musa returned to the Western Sudan with Muslim scholars from the Middle East, and subsequently built great mosques at Gao and Timbuctu on the Niger River. These cities became important Muslim centers. The famous Muslim traveler, Ibn Batutta from Morocco, visited Mali during the reign of *Mansa Musa's* successor and found it to be a secure and prosperous kingdom.

As Mali's prosperity declined toward the end of the fourteenth century, a new state rose to preeminence: Songhai. Early traditions place the founding of the Songhai state in the seventh century along the Niger River. Around 1300, new rulers with the title of *Sunni* appeared among the Songhai. The greatest of these rulers was *Sunni Ali*, the hero of the expansion of the empire, including his conquest of the famous city of Timbuctu in the heart of the old Mali Empire. Like Sundiata, Sunni Ali appears to have been a nominal Muslim, who may even have persecuted some of the Muslim clerics of Timbuctu. Perhaps for this reason, he had a poor reputation among the Islamic scholars, who may have plotted against him even during his lifetime. Such plotting led to the overthrow of Sunni Ali's son and successor and the establishment of a new powerful, strictly Islamic dynasty, that of the *Askias*. (*Askia* appears to have been a military title originally.)This new ruler was *Askia Muhammed the Great* who became the *Khalifa* (Caliph or Deputy) of the Western Sudan following his Hajj to Mecca in 1496 or 1497. He is known to have led a jihad, or Muslim holy war, against some other African states south of the Niger River. The Empire of Songhai reached its greatest extent (and the greatest extent of any of the great West

African empires) during the great *Askia's* reign, extending certainly into the area of the Hausa people in Northern Nigeria.

The history of these states shows the increasing power and influence of Islam as we move from the time of Ghana up to the period of the great empire of Songhai. The coup of the *Askias* reveal the political role that Muslims could play in the largest of the African states of that time.

Kanem-Borno

Around the shores of Lake Chad, in the northeast part of modern Nigeria, another powerful Sudanic African empire developed: the state now known as Kanem-Borno. Arabic sources refer to a state of Kanem as early as 872. The *Kanembu* people established a hegemony over the trade routes in the central Sudanic area in the ninth century in the area called Kanem, to the east of Lake Chad. These trade routes ran from Lake Chad north to the shores of Libya on the Mediterranean Sea and east across the savannahs to the Nile, providing a link with Egypt and the Middle East. By the 1000s, a divine king, known as the *Mai*, was ruling in Kanem. A Muslim gained control of the state and became the *Mai* sometime between 1075 and 1085. This man, known as *Mai* Hummay, established the dynasty known as the *Saifwa*, a name taken from that of an early Muslim hero, probably in an attempt to reinforce the family's Islamic links. Linguistic evidence indicates that the *Kanembu* and other African peoples of the region did not come from the Middle East but had been in or near their present location for many centuries. By the 1100s, there are reports of a *Mai* making at least two pilgrimages to Mecca, establishing more links with the Middle East. Despite the national conversion to Islam, certain non-Islamic practices, such as secluding the *Mai* from the gaze of the people, were retained until well into the nineteenth century.

The early Kanem empire reached the height of its power in the thirteenth century. By the middle of that century, the *Mais* had extended their influence into what is today southern Libya and west as far as the Hausa state of Kano in Nigeria. Diplomatic relations were established with Tunisia (a part of the Turkish Ottoman Empire) on the Mediterranean coast. The economic base of the state was trade in slaves; Kanem was too far east to have access to the gold that fueled the trade of Ghana, Mali, and Songhai. Following this brief period of expansion, Kanem declined into a period of anarchy and internal strife, leading the dynasty to relocate across Lake Chad in the Borno region of modern-day Nigeria, hence the identification of the empire later by the name, Kanem-Borno. The dominant people were displaced by a new group, called the *Kanuri*, who probably developed from a combination of Kanembu and other African peoples in the area. Stability was established around 1470, and a new walled capital was constructed.

The state then embarked on a second period of expansion; the old region of Kanem was re-occupied and a flourishing trade with Egypt developed. The most famous and powerful of all the *Mais* came to the throne in 1569 or 1570; this ruler was *Mai* ldris Alooma, who, like *Askia* Muhammed, inherited the title of *Khalifa*, which you will recall is a Muslim title for a representative of the successor of the prophet.[2] This *Mai* established direct diplomatic relations with the Turkish capital of Istanbul and launched several jihads against neighboring states and people. One such jihad took him to the gates of the Hausa city of Kano, which he besieged. Muslim clerics and teachers (known as the *ulama*) became extremely influential during the reign of *Mai* Idris Alooma.

The Islamic Kanuri people of northeastern Nigeria remain one of the most important ethnic groups in Northern Nigeria today. The writer, Zaynab Alkali, for example, is a member of this ethnic group. *The Stillborn*, her novel of life during the colonial period of Nigeria, reveals that even after long centuries of Islamic influence, there were still vestiges of ancestral religion in the rural areas of Borno. The grandmother of the novel's central character is clearly a practitioner of the older faith, while the younger generation is probably only nominally Muslim. The novelist suggests that Islam has had more influence in urban rather than rural areas over the years.

The Hausa States

The western half of northern Nigeria came to be dominated by the ethnic group called the Hausa, whose language, as we have seen, belongs to a branch of the Afroasiatic family. The Hausa developed a number of small but powerful city-states that participated in the Sudanic trading networks. Located between the areas dominated by Mali and Songhai on the one side and Kanem-Borno, on the other, Hausa cities were nearly always dominated by one or the other of the great empires.

The Hausa cities were founded sometime around 1000. Traditions suggest that the founding hero was a "King of Baghdad" who came to the area, killed a giant snake that blocked people's access to water, and married a local queen of the town of Daura. This king's son had six sons, who in turn became the first kings of Daura, Kano, Zaria, Gobir, Katsina, and Rano; the son of a daughter became the king of a smaller Hausa city. These became the original seven Hausa *Bakwai*, or states. Of the seven, only four had a significant impact on West African history: Kano, Katsina, Zaria, and Gobir.

Founding myths of this sort are not unusual in Africa. They may refer to vaguely remembered events—such as a small group of newcomers establishing their rule through conquest and marriage. The linguistic evidence, however, indicates that the Hausa people have been in the current location for a very long time, calling into question the historical reality of their migrating from the East or elsewhere. Traditions of this sort may rather represent an effort to legitimize political claims by basing them on Islamic heroes or traditions.

The Hausa were early town-dwellers, setting them apart from most African peoples, who lived in villages or small family-based compounds. Towns were located near sources of iron ore and on defensible sites. Towns that gave access to trade routes became important local trade centers for surrounding farmers. In fact, trade may have been the most important factor in the concentration of people in such towns. These towns grew into walled cities, becoming known as "*Birnin* Kano" or "*Birnin* Katsina," meaning "walled Kano" and "walled Katsina." Eventually, locally manufactured leather became a major item in trans-Saharan trade. "Moroccan" leather, in fact, came from the Hausa of northern Nigeria; it was called "Moroccan" because the usual European point of purchase was Morocco.

Islam came into the Hausa states with traders from Mali and Kanem-Borno. Mandinke traders from Mali were especially influential in the spreading of Islam into Hausaland and other parts of West Africa. Tradition maintains that the eleventh ruler of Kano converted to Islam between 1350 and 1385. In the 1400s, Muhammed Rumfa, the *Sarki* (ruler) of Kano, was known as a staunch Muslim. He sought the advice of an important Muslim cleric, al-Maghili, who wrote the book *The Obligation of Princes* for Muhammed Rumfa. *The Chronicle of Kano*, written by Muslim scholars, praises this Hausa ruler as a builder of mosques and enforcer of Muslim law.

Early Forest Kingdoms of West Africa

South of the great bend of the Niger River, traders from the Sudanic belt sought to organize the peoples of the forests to facilitate their trading. The largest states or kingdoms were developed in the following areas:

- the vicinity of modern Ghana, Ivory Coast, and Togo—the region of the *Akan* states;

- the region of southwestern Nigeria—the area of the Yoruba and Edo peoples;

- and an area directly west of Nigeria, among speakers of the *Fon* language, traditionally the state of Dahomey (but on the modern map, the Republic of Benin).

In addition to the gold from the Akan areas, an important item of trade was the *kola nut*, which grows in the tropical regions from the modern Ivory Coast through Southern Nigeria. The kola trade is possibly very ancient. In the west of the region, the trade was dominated by Akan-speakers and Mandinke traders from Mali or Songhai. The people of Oyo and the Hausa came to dominate the kola trade further East in the region of modern Nigeria. The Hausa traders also became quite important in the East-West trade in kola nuts running from the Volta River region of the Akan people to Hausaland. The long-distance trade required considerable skill and organization, because the nuts, if allowed to dry out, lost their value, taste, and texture. In novels of Chinua Achebe, especially the classic *Things Fall Apart*, the kola nut is shown to be an important part of traditional Igbo hospitality. The Muslim traders from the North valued it as one of the few stimulants not prohibited by the Koran. The high caffeine content kept caravan traders awake and alert during their long journeys. Kola eventually became a key ingredient, obviously, in American soft drinks.

The Akan States

Akan languages are spoken throughout the area of the modern nations of Ghana and the Ivory Coast. The Akan states were smaller than were the Sudanic kingdoms because the dense vegetation and the tse-tse flies of the forest prevented the use of cavalry. Although the areas were small, the populations were denser than in the Sudanic belt.

In the 1480s Europeans appeared at the coast of West Africa, learned of alluvial gold deposits and named the area of the Akan peoples "The Gold

Coast." These newcomers represented a new and much greater opportunity for trade than had the Muslims from the north, so there was a reorientation from the desert to the north to the Atlantic to the south. By 1750, most of the Akan states had been absorbed by two rival kingdoms: the Ashanti (or Asante) in the central part of modern-day Ghana, and the Fanti near the coast, both seeking access to the lucrative Atlantic trade. Eventually, the Ashanti kingdom became dominant—powerful enough to fight several wars with the British in the 1800s. By that time, Hausa traders from the area of Nigeria had established themselves in trading compounds in parts of the Akan-speaking area, even in the capital of the Ashanti Empire.

Oyo and Benin

The pattern of the Akan states was repeated to the East in the region of southwestern Nigeria. Although for convenience we refer to the kingdoms in this area as "forest" kingdoms, in fact the dense forest was broken in the area in which the great empire of Oyo developed. Oyo consequently had many features in common with the Sudanic kingdoms, such as dependence upon cavalry for their military might.

The largest empires in this area of Nigeria were formed by the Yoruba and Edo peoples. Both groups traditionally trace their history to the ancient Yoruba city of *Ife*, which was a spiritual center for both the Yoruba and Edo in historic times. Radiocarbon dates at archaeological digs showing remains of glass works suggest that Ife became a settlement of considerable size between the ninth and twelfth centuries. The impressive bronze sculptures of Ife indicate a trading link with the Sudanic belt, which would have supplied the necessary copper.

The founder of the city of Ife was said to be *Oduduwa*, one of the Yoruba *orishas*, a term for deities. Oduduwa descended from heaven on a golden chain, sprinkling sand from a sack to make dry land appear on the surface of the vast waters. A rooster, which he had also brought from heaven, scratched and scattered the land into hills, valleys, and islands. Then Oduduwa jumped down, landing on the spot that became Ife, the center of the earth, there to reign as the first *Oni*, the title for the ruler Ife. The name of the city, *Ile Ife*, can be translated as "original home of that which is wide," or origin of the earth (*Ile* means original or original home). Traditional belief is that a son or grandson of Oduduwa sent sons from Ife to found the royal dynasties of the various Yoruba kingdoms and the Benin kingdom of the related Edo people.[3] The general word for chief or ruler at any level among the Yoruba is *"oba,"* but specific *obas* generally have titles that include the name of the city or state over which they rule. *Oni* is hence probably a shortened version of *Onife* (ruler of Ife).

Oyo became one of the most powerful of African empires. Radiocarbon dates indicate a settlement there as early as 1100, with a sizable urban population by 1400. Oyo is sometimes translated from Yoruba as "slippery place," because the horse of the founder is said to have slipped on the ground on the side of the hill that became the original site of Oyo (*Oyo Ile,* "original Oyo"). Although some traditions trace the founding of the city back to the son of Oduduwa, *Shango* was the legendary founder in other myths. In some versions, Shango was a son or grandson of Oduduwa and a prince from the neighboring kingdom of Nupe, north of Oyo. Such traditions suggest a connection between the ruling families of Ife and Nupe in the founding of Oyo. Oyo reached its zenith during the seventeenth and eighteenth centuries. During that time, Oyo dominated all the people in the open country down to the coast. The ruler, or *oba*, of Oyo took the title, *Alafin*, which means ruler of the "palace," which in Yoruba is *"afin."*

Oyo's expansion into an empire no doubt owes its inception to involvement in the long-distance trans-Saharan trade. Like Ife and even Benin, it was conveniently located both for defense and as trade terminus. As was the case with the Akan states, however, the appearance of new traders on the ocean—the Europeans—provided a new impetus for expanding control over trade routes. Indeed, the greatest power of Oyo followed contact with European trade and probably derives from the prosperity such contact made possible.

This trade eventually was dominated by slavery as the Europeans sought to provide cheap labor for sugar plantations in the New World. Oyo and other African trading kingdoms became enmeshed in the Atlantic slave trade, as we will see in a later section of this text. Power increasingly was based on access to the guns and other European products the slave trade provided. The coast of the area of *Dahomey,* subordinate to the Oyo Empire nearly into the nineteenth century, was called the "Slave Coast" by the European sailors.

Oyo[4] was by far the largest and most powerful of the Yoruba states, covering perhaps 10,000 square miles. It and the other Yoruba states are discussed further in the next chapter. *Benin,* although small in area because of its location in dense forest, was also powerful, and home to an artistic tradition of world importance—the famous Benin bronzes. Some art historians see similarity between these bronze sculptures and the terra cotta heads of the ancient Nok culture. The kingdom of Benin was founded by the Edo people, whose language is quire similar to those of the Yoruba and Igbo, their western and eastern neighbors, respectively.

The foundations of Benin are unclear. An *Oba* succeeded in becoming paramount over other village leaders and chiefs sometime around 1200–1300. According to legend, the Edo people sent to Oduduwa at Ife, asking for a king to rule over them. Historically, these traditions indicate a connection through Ife between Yoruba and Edo traditions. Possibly in a secession crisis or other local dispute, the Edo sent to Ife for a compromise ruler, or the tradition may indicate a conquest of the area of Benin by leaders from Ife, with the story added later about their having been invited to rule.

Having succeeded in enhancing his power at the expense of the council of nobles, the fourth *Oba* renamed the state *Ubini* (or Benin). Thereafter the people of this kingdom are referred to as *Bini* rather than the more general term, Edo. Members of this ruling dynasty are credited with the introduction of bronze casting from Ife, new kinds of weapons, and horses. The wealth necessary to support Benin's elaborate art and court traditions probably came from its trans-Saharan trading interests.

An *Oba* named *Ewuare*, remembered as the greatest ruler of Benin, embarked on a series of conquests that made Benin into an empire in the 1400s. He extended control over some Igbo as well as some of the eastern Yoruba states. Art flourished at Benin in this period (1504–1550), a sort of "colony" was established at Lagos, and the first contact was made with Europeans at the coast. (Lagos was called Eko by the Yoruba, hence the traditional ruler of the city was the *Eleko*. The name, Lagos, derives from the Portuguese name for the area, *Lago de Curamo*). The Portuguese established diplomatic relations with Benin, and Bini ambassadors were dispatched to Lisbon, Rome and some other European cities. Trade was reoriented toward the Atlantic rather than the north, and the slave trade became important in that commerce.

Small-Scale Societies of Southern Nigeria

In many parts of Africa, people were not organized into large-scale states or kingdoms. European administrators during the colonial period referred to these small-scale societies as "stateless." Scholars today contend that the distinction between African states and "stateless" peoples is somewhat misleading. Most Africans found their lives organized quite similarly whether they were technically subjects of an empire, such as Mali or Oyo, or were residents of "stateless" societies as were the Igbo of Nigeria. Everyday life took place largely within the village and near environs, while outward-directed pursuits such as trade or warfare were sporadic and only temporary. People in small-scale communities lived ordered lives within the regulated system so neatly detailed in Achebe's *Things Fall Apart*. Some estimates place the number of small scale societies among the Igbo at 2,700.

Along the coast of the Atlantic small communities of various ethnic groups were located on the creeks, inlets, and lagoons of the delta country where the people lived by fishing and gathering salt. These small communities were in a good position to take advantage of trading opportunities when the European ships appeared off the coast in the fifteenth and sixteenth centuries. Some grew into small trading cities engaged in the Atlantic slave trade and, later, in the palm oil trade with the Europeans. The cities were dominated by large trading "houses" managed by the heads of important families with their retainers, supporters, and slaves. In each city three or four such houses organized the trade with English, French, Portuguese, and other European traders. Secret societies provided connections among the leaders and traders of the houses in the various cities and towns of the coast. These secret societies, with rituals of initiation and festivals, providing links among the houses and cities that allowed for coordination among the Africans in their dealings with the Europeans.

The Igbo

The people of the hinterland constituted one of the largest ethnic groups in Nigeria (and in Africa, for that matter): the Igbo. The Igbo, whose language is part of the large *Kwa* sub-family of West Africa, are located at the eastern edge of the *Kwa*-speaking group. Like the other *Kwa* speakers, the Igbo are part of the Yam Complex, indicating an affinity with other West African peoples of the coastal region of West Africa.

Igbo people are found on both sides of the Niger River, although the majority is on the eastern side. Those on the western side, probably influenced by Benin and similar kingdoms, did establish some large-scale states or kingdoms. On the eastern side, however, small-scale, village-based societies predominate. The Igbo have one of the densest rural populations in Africa, almost 1,000 people to the square mile. Archaeological finds of pottery from 5,000 years ago resemble pottery made by modern Igbo. Such artifacts, together with linguistic evidence, suggest that the Igbo are a very ancient people in southeastern Nigeria. The Igbo were making widespread use of iron tools by the first century. Major growth and expansion of the Igbo population seems to have occurred from the ninth century onwards, as they gradually spread out from a central core area over the region that they occupy today.

Summary

Our brief historical overview of the context in which the cultures of West Africa developed clearly points to a high level of social, political, and artistic sophistication in existence long before the coming of the Europeans. The most important catalyst for further development was probably international trade, beginning with the long-distance caravan trade in the north which brought to Nigeria an international religion, Islam. With Islam came a writing script, Arabic, and Islamic patterns of social and political organization, particularly among the Hausa and the Kanuri of Kanem-Borno. In southern Nigeria, the international trade route shifted orientation from the Sudanic North to the Atlantic, along which eventually traveled not only goods and slaves but new ideas as well. The peoples of the forest, or *Guinea*, region developed both centralized states and small-scale, village-based societies. The area of the *Kwa*-speaking people, encompassing the area of the "Yam Complex," stretched from the Akan areas in the West to the Yoruba, Edo and Igbo peoples in Nigeria. The Hausa traders eventually established themselves as far away as the Akan empire of Ashanti. The Yoruba and Edo, traditionally town dwellers, organized some of the more powerful centralized kingdoms of West Africa, notably the empires of Oyo and Benin. Most of the Igbo, despite their dense population, did not develop monarchies nor even traditions or histories standard throughout all Igbo areas. Clearly, ethnic and linguistic similarities, as shown among the people of southern Nigeria, do not necessarily lead to similar political and social structures.

References

1. Lester Brookes (1971). *Great Civilizations of Ancient Africa*. New York: Four Winds Press, p. 137.

2. "Alooma" (pronounced "ah-lome-ah") was actually applied to his name after his death in a battle in a swamp called *"Aloo."*

3. The seven sons of Oduduwa, sent out from Ife according to legend, became the Oba of Benin, the Olowa of Owu, the Orangun of Ila, the Alafin of Oyo, the Onisabe of Sabe, the Olupopo of Popo, and the Alaketu of Ketu.

4. A list of some of the other Yoruba states in the forest belt will indicate the complexity of the actual situation: Ijebu, to the south of Oyo; Owu, which was
often subordinate to Oyo; Owo, which was often in the Benin sphere of influence; Ilorin, in the north, was eventually part of the Muslim Fulani empire;
Ondo, which refers to "settlers" from the Oduduwa tradition; and the Ijesha
state. Abeokuta was founded by the Egba branch of Yoruba in the Nineteenth
Century as the old Oyo empire fell apart. The powerful kingdom of Ibadan
had similar origins in the 1800s.

CHAPTER THREE

Traditional Societies of Nigeria

One cannot yet speak of a "Nigerian" culture or national identity. There are as many as 250 different ethnic cultures within the boundaries of the modern Republic of Nigeria. Still, three ethnic groups have become dominant in each of three geographical areas of the country—the Hausa in the north, the Yoruba in the southwest, and the Igbo in the southeast. Today, these three peoples represent some of the largest ethnic groups in all of Africa. The focus of this text is consequently on the traditions of these three groups. Remember, however, that these ethnic identifications are relatively recent themselves. Many people now designated Hausa, for example, may not traditionally have thought of themselves in those terms.

Although we know more about the history of the Hausa and the Yoruba than about that of the Igbo, recent anthropological study provides us with significant information concerning the traditional way of life among the Igbo as well as the other two peoples. Although the traditions described here are presented as aspects of the historical past, the reader should bear in mind that African tradition remains vital in the modern world.

The Importance of Kinship

These three peoples, like many other African groups, placed great importance on kinship in organizing their societies. Lines of kinship were used for establishing one's identity, role, and obligations within the community. Two features of kinship organization are particularly important in understanding how these systems worked. The first is the principle of unilineal descent. Americans have some difficulty in identifying ancestors back through very many generations because we trace descent through both parents—so we have four grandparents, eight great-parents, sixteen great great-grandparents, and so on. In a system of unilineal descent, ancestors are traced only through fathers or mothers, not both—so one would have two grandparents, two great-grandparents, and so on. The second feature was a consequence of the widespread practice of polygyny, which resulted in many half-brothers and half-sisters who were, however, related through the *lineage* (the people tracing descent from a common ancestor through unilineal descent).

Several lineages could be related to some more distant ancestor, which resulted in an identification sometimes called a *clan*, although this term tends to be loosely applied. "Tribe," or ethnic group, is an amalgamation of all the lineages and clans sharing a common language, culture, and often, religious beliefs and practices.

Africans are and have been overwhelmingly rural, living in farming communities or compounds. Typically, the household comprises a man and one or several wives, their children, other relatives, such as grandparents, aunts, or uncles, and clients—people who for one reason or another are not attached to a specific family group. In some areas in past times, there also would have been clients who could be described as slaves associated with the family compound (war captives, hostages, ritually-designated slaves, purchased slaves, or others). Family relationships, then, tended to be more complex than is the case with the smaller, nuclear families now associated with American living styles.

An individual was therefore identified as a member of several kinship groups—a family, a lineage, and a clan. In addition, other groups provided identity and demanded some allegiance or loyalty. For example, young people of approximately the same age from a particular area, lineage, or ethnic group might be thought of as constituting one such identifiable group. Often, these young people underwent a period of instruction and initiation together, which resulted in their developing a special loyalty to each other across kinship lines. Other age groups were possible bases for identification as well. For a particular set of years, a man was a warrior, then a junior elder, then a senior elder, and so on.

Marriage outside one's own lineage or clan (a practice referred to as exogamy; endogamy is marriage within a specified group) also resulted in in-law obligations and loyalties that cut across direct kinship lines. Exogamy was often required; marriage to a "relative" within the lineage was not permitted.

People in African cultures may be thought of as both belonging *in* and belonging *to* specified kinship groups. "Belonging to" implies that the group had some authority over that individual and that he or she owed definite obligations to the group. An individual without such ties would be considered an outsider or stranger, with no rights and with no protection. Describing his own people, Victor Uchendu writes that an Igbo without a patrilineage "is an Igbo without citizenship."[1] Traditionally, an African had rights and freedoms only as part of a body or community. American notions of individualism would seem strange and unfamiliar in these contexts.

Within its boundaries, Nigeria exhibits significant ethnic complexity. In addition to Hausa, Igbo, and Yoruba, there are many smaller, distinct peoples as well. The three largest groups, which serve as the foci of this text, do not comprise the entire modern nation, a point which can easily be forgotten when thinking of Nigeria's ethnic relations of today. The pastoral Fulani people, who follow their herds through lands otherwise occupied by other ethnic groups, add an additional complexity in the north. This text has already alluded to other important ethnic groups as well: the Kanuri in the northeast, the Edo of the Benin Empire in southern Nigeria, the Nupe, who may have been involved in the founding of the early dynasty of Oyo, and the coastal peoples such as the Ijo and Ibibio, located between the Igbo and the Atlantic Ocean. As the table on the following page reveals, the three largest groups today comprise over two-thirds of the population of Nigeria; the seven largest groups account for fully 85 percent. Together with closely related peoples, these ethnic groups total over 93 percent of the nation's population, currently estimated at 131 million people. With that in mind, we now turn to discussion of the traditions of each of the major three ethnic groups.

The Hausa

Authorities question whether there is or has been a uniform Hausa cultural identity. The term seems to refer more to a collection of peoples speaking the Hausa language, while exhibiting many variations in life style, world view, and value system. Hausa has become a *lingua franca* (a widespread second language often used for commercial purposes) throughout a wide area of the West Africa. Some estimates place the number of Hausa speakers today as high as 38 million, 32 million in northern Nigeria alone. Most other Hausa today live in the Republic of Niger north of Nigeria, who were artificially separated from Nigeria's Hausa by the borders the British and French drew to demarcate their respective spheres of influence during the colonial period. The Hausa language, which uses a form of Arabic script, provided a written literature in this part of West Africa long before European influences reached the region. The impact of modern institutions and political life has served to mold a Hausa culture more uniform today than that which probably existed in earlier history.

Table 1. Peoples of Nigeria

Largest Identifiable Ethnic Groups

Total Population: 131 million (2006 est.)

Ethinc Group	Percent of Population
Hausa-Fulani	29.0%
Yoruba	21.0%
Igbo	18.0%
Ijaw	10.0%
Kanuri	4.0%
Ibibio	3.5%
Tiv	3.5%

The Hausa have long identified closely with the Islamic religion which came to Hausaland in the fourteenth century. Historically, the Hausa have adhered to the Sunni branch of Islam and followed the Maliki school of law. Islam brought the Hausa in touch with an international civilization with an institutionalized legal system, writing, literature, and architecture. Hausa children typically studied in Koranic schools with a teacher called a *mallam* (boys still receive much more such education than girls). The mallams often dispensed protective medicines and charms, as well. For example, the water used to wash a Koranic verse or chapter from a board was thought to have talismanic effects. The *mallams* were maintained by *zakat* (charity, one of the Five Pillars, or requirements, of Islam), but many of them had small farms, too.

As in the present day, men in Hausa communities of the past often belonged to one of the Muslim brotherhoods, called *tariqas*. Large numbers of Hausa have performed the *hajj* (in fact, the central government organizes airline flights to Mecca and Medina for this purpose today). The Hausa traditionally practiced some forms of female exclusion, although women were free to visit each other in the evenings and to visit relatives. They even carried on trade through the use of intermediaries.

The effects of the Islamic influence were far-reaching for the Hausa. They were brought into contact with a world history and tradition. The literacy brought by Arabic script allowed for the development of a written literature, record-keeping for a bureaucracy as well as for business, and an external, international set of values carried through the *Koran*, the *Shari'a* (the system of Islamic law), and the Muslim scholars and clerics. The Islamic presence also set up a continuing and often unresolved tension between the traditional beliefs and values of the Hausa and the newer, occasionally more militant values of the Muslim community. Movements of Islamic reform and fundamentalism, such as the Fulani jihads of the nineteenth century, often threatened to undermine the power of traditional Hausa rulers, even though they were themselves Muslims.

The economic base for each Hausa state depended upon factors such as location and history. For example, Gobir, as the northernmost of the states, was very much involved in the trans-Saharan trade through relationships with Songhai and Kanem-Borno, as well as with the Tuareg Berbers of the north. Kano and Katsina were more involved with the trade organized from the Mali and Songhai regions to their West. This long-distance and medium-distance trade took Hausa traders south to the Benue River region, east to Borno, and west as far as the Volta River region of the Akan-speakers. While the trade across the Sahara was carried on by use of camels, this southern trade along the fringes of the forest depended upon the donkey, oxen, and human porters. The Hausa were also adept at the canoe-borne trade on the Niger River. This involvement in trade led to the important profession of the caravan-leader among the Hausa. Historians speak of a Hausa "diaspora," or dispersion, as Hausa traders established camps, called *zongos*, as far west as the Ashanti Empire in modern-day Ghana.

Throughout historical times, the Hausa were divided among several social classes. At the top of the hierarchy were the ruling class, made up of the "chiefs," or *Sarakuna* (singular, *Sarki*) and courtiers. The Muslim scholars, judges, teachers and wealthy merchants were politically and socially prominent. Then there were the urban populations of the towns and cities, both free and slave, and the people of the countryside, who were both free peasants and agricultural slaves, some of whom lived in slave villages or worked on large farms owned by the rulers, courtiers, or wealthy merchants. On the margins of the Hausa society were the pastoral nomads living in Fulani cattle encampments. Most of the members of the ruling class considered themselves Muslims. Town dwellers included craftsmen, shopkeepers, small merchants, and the like, as well as some beggars and the poor (in Islamic countries, beggars are not necessarily poor; in Kano, some were reciters of poems and songs who received fairly good incomes from alms).

In the rural areas, essentially the entire adult male population is still today engaged in farming as the primary occupation, particularly cultivating sorghum and millet for food. Low average population density allows for generally widespread access to adequate farm land. The work is very labor intensive, since most work is done with the hoe as the only tool or machinery. Ox-drawn plows are fairly rare, and tractors rarer still. Each rural family lives in a compound with a compound head, normally the oldest adult male. Men primarily are responsible for field work, while women's primary duties lie in child-rearing, housework, threshing and grinding grain, and cooking. The growing acceptance of the Islamic practice of *purdah* (secluding women) further restricts women's occupation outside the home.[2]

Marriage is nearly universal and virtually obligatory. Roles for single persons, such as bachelor, nun, or unmarried priest, simply do not exist. Pressure is exerted on women, particularly, to marry quite young and to stay married. Over half the women are married by age 14 and nearly 100 percent by age 19. Young widows and divorcees are seen as having a duty to get remarried, or they risk being perceived as prostitutes.[3] Men are under intense pressure to marry as well but not at such a young age. As in many parts of Nigeria, and Africa in general, marriage is a public, family matter, not a private arrangement between two individuals. The giving of bridewealth (an exchange of property from the groom's family to that of the bride) constitutes the visible or tangible sign of the contractual obligations marriage creates between two family groups or compounds. Polygamy is acceptable and even encouraged given the pressure on women to be married and the typical surplus of women of marriageable age over the number of available adult males.

Historically, in both town and rural areas, there were different categories of slaves, reminding us that in non-Western countries the concept of slavery is much more complex than in American experience. For example, some were born into their status but were servants of powerful chiefs and kings and could wield considerable influence in their own right. One of the early Kings of Mali began his career as such a slave. There were house slaves, essentially domestic servants, who were often considered nearly members of the family. In the countryside were the inhabitants of so-called slave villages, who worked for absentee farm-owners, but also had the right to own and work their own farm plots as well. Some scholars have suggested their status was more like that of the serfs of Russia rather than of slaves. Usually these kinds of slaves were not those transported across the Sahara in the slave trade. This trade appears to have depended upon war captives or others captured in raids on surrounding peoples.

In Kano, crafts were particularly important, such as cloth weaving, cloth dyeing, and leather working. Still, most Hausa were farmers, often living within the walls of the towns or cities and going out to till their fields in the day. Living within the area of the "Cereal Complex," they cultivated millet and sorghum as primary grain crops. During long dry seasons, the farmers often turned to crafts for supplemental income. In modern times, they have added cultivation of cash crops, such as groundnuts (peanuts) and cotton.

While there were rivalries among the various states, no one of them was able to subdue the others, so there was no overarching Hausa Empire. As wealth from long-distance trade became more important, however, intra-Hausa rivalry appears to have been exacerbated. As warfare spread among the states, taxation increased, as did the growing sense of separation between the Hausa elite and the common people. These changes provide an important background to the revolutions that spread throughout Hausaland in the nineteenth century as a result of the Fulani jihads, or holy wars.

The association between Hausa and Fulani became so close in northern Nigeria in the nineteenth century that many scholars now speak of the Hausa-Fulani as a single ethnic group. This seeming amalgamation resulted from the fact that Fulani became the ruling class over many of the Hausa states during the upheavals of that century. Other pastoral Fulani gave up herding because of drought and cattle diseases in the last century, and became cultivators alongside the Hausa. In both cases, the Fulani tended to lose their original language and became "Hausa-ized."

Still, distinct Fulani Populations remain throughout West Africa and even in parts of Nigeria. As a matter of fact, the Fulani of West Africa, according to one authority, "form the largest nomadic society in the world."[4] They and their herds (cattle and sheep) stretch across the Sudan from east of Lake Chad all the way to the Atlantic Ocean in Senegal. "Fulani," the term used for these people in English, is from the Hausa word for them; they call themselves the *Fulbe* (plural; singular, *Peul*; language, *Fulfulde*). The Hausa rulers allowed them to have grazing rights as they moved within or across the territories of Kano, Katsina, Gobir, or Zaria. They were organized under their own clan chiefs, however. There was, of course, potential conflict between the Hausa farmers and the Fulani herders, because cattle could trample or eat crops and farmers could enclose grazing land. The Hausa rulers also instituted a cattle-tax resented by the Fulani herders. Such resentments of taxes and land enclosures could underlie the animosities brought to the surface in the Fulani jihads of the early 1800s.

The Fulani can be subdivided into the herding, nomadic branch (rural Fulani), and the scholarly, urban branch. These latter Fulani became prominent in Islamic affairs, especially in Nigeria among the Hausa. Usually, these Fulani scholars and clerics were members of the *Qadiriyya* brotherhood. It is this last group that led the jihads in the nineteenth century and became the ruling elite of the Hausa; they usually speak Hausa and no longer the *Fulfulde* language.

The Yoruba

The term Yoruba originally referred to the inhabitants of the great empire of Oyo. Eventually, the name came to be applied to all the people of southwestern Nigeria speaking the same language as the people of Oyo. We should note that, as is the case for the Hausa, the Yoruba today represent a more homogeneous group than was probably the case in the past. We have seen that the Yoruba trace their political and religious identity to the city-state of Ife, which was believed to have been the center of the world, the point where the divine being, Oduduwa, first made dry (habitable) land. From Ife the rulers of the various Yoruba states, as well as of Benin, were sent out.

While today Yoruba are scattered throughout communities all over West Africa, about 17 million reside in the southwestern area of Nigeria. Some Yoruba-speakers also live in the neighboring Republic of Benin (formerly Dahomey), as the British and French boundary makers in colonial times divided the area between them. While the common people known as Yoruba have probably lived in this general vicinity for thousands of years, the legends regarding rulers coming from Ife may indicate a class of invaders from the North (from the Sudan, perhaps) who established their hegemony over the Yoruba.

Traditionally, the Yoruba were town or city dwellers, with smaller farming communities associated with each town or city. The towns were made up of a combination of large family compounds (each compound housing as many as 1,000 people). The compounds were organized around and based upon kinship. The lineages held the farm land in common in areas beyond the boundaries of the town itself. This feature of living in a town some distance from one's farm is distinctive of the Yoruba. Each town at its center had an "*Afin,*" the dwelling place for the town's *oba*, or chief. The *oba* was seen as the townspeople's priest and protector, which could explain the settlement around his residence.

The Yoruba share some distinctive religious beliefs that allow for toleration of newer religions. Today about one-half of the Yoruba of Nigeria are Muslim and many are Christian, but they often feel welcome and comfortable at ceremonies or rituals celebrating the Yoruba traditional beliefs. These traditional beliefs vary from place to place and from time to time; nevertheless, most versions see the universe as consisting of a domain of the sky above and one of the earth beneath, with the habitable world in between.

The domain of the sky is under the dominion of *Olorun Oludumare* ("*Olorun*" means "sky-owner"). *Olorun* is remote from the affairs of people and therefore not prayed to or invoked to meet human needs. The domain of the earth (referring to the earth that supports the cultivable or inhabited part of the visible world) is represented by a female deity, *Onilo* (earth-owner), but more usually called *Ile* (the personification of earth); often she is invoked as *Iya*, "Mother." It is she who receives the souls of the dead.

Beneath *Olorun*, the ruler of the sky, are the various *orishas*, which may also be referred to as "gods." It is these *orishas* who involve themselves in affairs of the world. There are principal *orishas*, who are heads of lineages of lesser *orishas*—so they are arranged hierarchically. Some of the major *orishas* include the following: *Oduduwa*, as we have seen, the founder of Ife and Yoruba culture; *Shango*, associated with thunder and lightning and the personal *orisha* of the kings of Oyo; *Ogun*, the *orisha* of iron-working (as well as of warriors, barbers, and others whose work depends upon iron); and *Oya*, the female *orisha* who is thought of as the wife of *Shango* and associated with the River Niger. While these *orishas*, among others, are seen as being part of the sky domain, other *orishas* are thought of as operating especially in the world of people, for example, *Ifa*, the *orisha* of divination; and *Eshu*, the trickster, associated with market places. Those who specialized in divination, through the *orisha* called *Ifa* were the *babalawo*. *Ifa* divination involved casting kola nuts or strings of beads and then interpreting the patterns. *Eshu* might also be invoked, and so an image of *Eshu* sometimes appears on the carved wooden tray on which the kola nuts are cast.

In addition to the *orishas*, there are also beings of the sky, who are the spirit doubles of all those people living on the earth or waiting to be born. Many Yoruba consider sub-set of sky people to be the source for the "bad" children, who die in infancy over and over again, tormenting their mothers.

This belief is very likely a folk explanation for the high infant mortality among the people of the tropical regions of West Africa. As we shall see, the Igbo of southeastern Nigeria have a similar explanation for the existence of these "bad" children.

In addition to these beings, the spirits from the earth below, called the *Ogboni*, were *Ile's* (earth's) counterparts to the *orishas* of *Olorun* (the sky). Often, the *Ogboni* seemed to be vengeful spirits, perhaps representing the ancestors among some Yoruba. *Egungun*, the Masks, usually represented sanctions of the ancestors taken against those who failed to uphold the traditions of the community.

There were cults for each of the major *Orishas*, for the *Ogboni* and for the *Egungun*. At Oyo, the *Ogboni* cult was especially important, since it mediated between the council of elders, known as the *Oyo Mesi*, and the ruler, the *Alafin*. The members of the *Ogboni* cult were often priests or elders in other cults, so they represented the important leaders throughout Oyo society. The cult of *Shango* was especially important in Oyo because he was thought of as an *Alafin* who had been deified. The *Alafins* made use of the cult of *Shango* in collecting fees for purification rites throughout Yorubaland and relied upon respect for the cult in extending their power. The *Egungun* cult was also powerful because the masks were the method by which powerful ancestors and some gods were called upon to settle the town's business. One of the most powerful of the *Egungun* was "owned" by the *Alafin*, which is to say that he kept the mask and assigned the person to wear the mask.

The organization of the universe, as envisioned by the Yoruba, was the basis for the organization of cities and states. Through various offices and cults, society was ordered to reflect the order of the Sky and the Earth.

Politically, the Yoruba were divided into several states of varying size and power, each consisting of several towns, each town with its own *oba*. As seen above, the state of Oyo was quite large, while among the branch of Yoruba called the Ekiti, states were extremely small. The leading *oba* in a capital of a state was permitted to wear a beaded crown, hence these capitals were called "crowned towns." The title of the leading *oba* generally came from the name of the town, as the *Olowo* of Owo, or the *Oni(fe)* of Ife, and the *Eleko* of Eko.

An *oba* usually led a life of ceremony and ritual, secluded in his *afin*. He was surrounded by a "cabinet" of leading hereditary chiefs. In Oyo, this powerful body was known as the *Oyo Mesi* (from the Yoruba for "Oyo knows the answers"). The *oba* was typically chosen from a particular royal male lineage. For example, in Oyo, the *Oyo Mesi* selected the *Alafin* from males in the royal family. Some states used divination to determine which member of a lineage would be *oba*. In certain areas, the *obas* had to meet certain physical standards. In one small Ekiti state, for example, a candidate could be rejected for being too tall, out of fear that he would look down on his subjects. Women were not necessarily excluded; there are traditions of female *obas* in some of the towns.

At Oyo, the *Alafin* did not usually go beyond the verandah of his palace except during the celebration of certain annual rituals. The palace household comprised several kinds of officials and attendants. An important official was the master of the horse, as represented by the character *Elesin* in Wole Soyinka's play, *Death and the King's Horseman*. He was among several officials expected to commit suicide upon the death of an *Alafin* in order to accompany the king on his journey into the afterlife. There were high-ranking eunuchs who often were stand-ins for the *Alafin* at various rituals. There was a group of royal slaves, marked by shaved heads, who served as bodyguards and messengers for the king. Another powerful group included the ladies of the court, led by the "*iya oba*," or official mother of the *Alafin*. (By comparison, the "mother of the market" in Soyinka's play mentioned above is called "*Iyaloja*".) The *Alafin's* actual mother would have been "invited to go to sleep" and buried when her son became the ruler. In addition were the many royal wives, or queens, and several other female court officials. Three relatives of the *Alafin*, including his son, titled the *Aremo*, would be designated as official "fathers of the king." The tradition developed in the 1700s that the *Aremo*, like the King's horseman, would also commit suicide on the death of the *Alafin*. The eldest son, therefore, could never inherit the throne.

The power of the Yoruba *obas*, including the *Alafin*, was restricted in several ways. The government in the Yoruba kingdoms appeared quite confusing to outsiders, no doubt because of the division of responsibilities and authority among so many competing groups. Oyo, because of its prominence, offers the best known example of divided rule. In that empire, the major check on the ruler's power was the *Oyo Mesi*, mentioned above, which was made up of seven councilors, each of whom held a hereditary title in his own family or lineage. This council had the power to announce the rejection of the *Alafin*, who on receiving such a message from the council, was obliged to commit suicide. The leader of the council was the *Bashorun*, the main kingmaker and interpreter of the divinations of the *Alafin's* personal spirit. At the height of Oyo's power, one of these *Bashoruns* became even more powerful than the *Alafins*, four of whom he had killed. During his "reign" an army of Oyo reportedly even defeated an army of the Ashanti in the West. In 1774, the fifth *Alafin* to come to power during this *Bashorun's* time succeeded in having him killed. This *Alafin*, Abiodun, reigned over a time of peace and prosperity, which was the calm before the storm of the decline of Oyo and the violent upheavals among the Yoruba of the nineteenth century. After the death of Abiodun in 1789, the famous Oyo cavalry was never as effective as it had been during his time.

Patrilineal descent groups, or lineages as described in the first section of this chapter, were the basic social organization of the Yoruba people. Because the lineages were patrilineal, women could not become heads of these groups, but in many Yoruba cities the women were represented in governmental councils by a woman chief, usually titled the *Iyalode*. Throughout much of West Africa, the local marketplaces were preeminently the sphere of the market women, who would be led by a woman such as the *Iyaloja*.

The major occupation of the people was farming, even though most were town dwellers. Many farmers also practiced various crafts such as weaving and working in iron or involved themselves in long-distance trade during seasons not conducive to farming.

Yoruba society included several categories of persons not considered free. In addition to slavery, there was a condition constituting a temporary pawning of a person or his or her child to pay off a debt or to raise money. As among the Hausa, royal slaves could become powerful civil or military servants. There were classes of slaves for working farms and serving in households as well. Also, as among the Hausa, slaves were acquired mainly as war captives, but criminals and debtors could also fall into this condition. Because warfare with other peoples produced so many of the slaves, many were non-Yoruba, which could be a destabilizing influence. Hausa slaves in Oyo's province of Ilorin seem to have provided the forces for the uprising against Oyo there during the time of the Fulani jihads, as described later in the next chapter.

The Igbo

As noted in regard to the Hausa and Yoruba, the Igbo probably had no overarching notion of an Igbo ethnic identity before very recent times.

Even today, some Igbo-speaking groups, especially those living west of the Niger River, reject the designation of Igbo. The word "Igbo," originally meaning "community of people" or "the people," acquired connotations suggesting "forest dwellers," "bush men," or "backwardness." Such connotations could have easily led to the rejection of the term among these people and other Igbo-speakers. The term only began to be accepted in the 1940s when a kind of national consciousness developed among the Igbo as they realized they had political and economic interests in common.[5]

The Igbo lived in small farming villages scattered throughout the densely forested region of southeastern Nigeria. For the most part, Igbo communities consisted of very small-scale societies. Kingship was rare among them, although not unknown. In the western part of Igboland, near the sphere of Benin, there was a kingdom with an Obi, or king (note the similarity with *Oba*). The position of *Obi* was not hereditary, however; he was elected from among the residents of certain villages. These elections are hotly contested even in the present day.

The typical Igbo polities were organized at two levels: the village and the village-group. Each village was essentially sovereign and ruled by direct participatory democracy. Three to six (occasionally more) villages in a small geographical area could also be associated in a village-group. The issues that the village group could take up were restricted by various kinds of traditional charters, or founding myths. In deliberations at this level, each village had equal representation and was required to make equal contributions to undertakings of the village-group. Important decisions usually required unanimity of all the villages. When they conquered this area, the British as well as other outsiders, were surprised to find so dense a population maintaining apparent order and stability without centralized political structures.

Villages comprised several compounds, each with a compound head who had some authority in areas of work assignments, ritual, and so on. Each compound consisted of several households which formed the extended family. Some compound heads were also lineage heads, and so had ritual functions that went with leadership of the lineage. Among the Igbo, the lineages were usually patrilineal.

The village rather than a centralized state, therefore, was the focus of politics, law, and order. Leadership positions within the village normally were held by titled men and women. Legislative functions were exercised by councils consisting of all adult males of the village. Everyone present could speak on any issue being debated, but following the discussion, the lineage heads would retire from the meeting room for a consultation. When the consultation was finished, the best orator among the heads would be selected to give the decision to the rest of the assembly. Issues dealt with could include regulating markets, setting prices, burning bush for farming purposes, or deciding on peace and war.

Legal cases often were handled by the same assembly of adult males. The assembly lacked any coercive function in enforcing its decisions, however. A man found guilty of murder, for example, was expected to hang himself—there was no community right to inflict capital punishment. The villagers could bring social pressure on the criminal, but that was all. If the culprit fled, his kinship group was expected to flee also and give up all its property. The effectiveness of these sanctions is illustrated in Achebe's novel, *Things Fall Apart*, in the actions of the main protagonist, Okonkwo. After accidentally shooting a relative, Okonkwo and his extended family immediately flee to his mother's home village. His good friends, after helping the family on their way, destroy Okonkwo's compound and all his property. No one tells him or his friends to take these actions: they all understand their obligations implicitly.

The Igbo world view envisioned interaction between the world of the living and the world of the "dead," or of the spirits. The second world included the ancestors as well as those who had not yet been born. The Igbo high god was, like *Olorun* of the Yoruba, withdrawn from the world, his creative work completed. There were various titles for the high god, depending upon the characteristic being emphasized. Often, this god was referred to as *Chukwu* (the Great God).

Below *Chukwu* were various nature gods. One of the most important of these was *Ala* or *Ani*, the earth goddess, who is closest to people of this world (compare *Ile* of the Yoruba). She was the great mother who must be appeased in any matter relating to land or the earth (such as the sale of property). Usually benevolent, *Ala* was responsible for punishing major offense, such as incest; one found to be guilty of such an offense was denied burial in the ground. There was also a sun god who helped crops and trees to grow.

Large rivers, such as the Niger, were felt to have spiritual force as well. In addition, there were spirits of forests and other places, spirit doubles for individuals, and the "bad" children mentioned earlier in the discussion of traditional beliefs of the Yoruba. Called *ogbanje*, they would die in infancy or early childhood only to be reborn and die again. This belief is illustrated in Achebe's *Things Fall Apart*. The favorite daughter of Okonkwo, the main character, is thought to be an *ogbanje*. A spiritual healer, however, succeeded in having the daughter lead him to the secret, buried charm that connected her to the spirit world of the *ogbanje*, and thereby ended the cycle. As noted earlier, such a belief probably represents an attempt to explain the high rate of infant mortality along the West African coast where malaria is endemic.

Comparable to the *Egungun* cults among the Yoruba were *Egwugwu* cults among the Igbo. The *Egwugwu* appeared among the Igbo often to help resolve disputes or to deal with those accused of wrongdoing. This practice is again well-described by Achebe in his novel of traditional Igbo life. In one chapter, the *Egwugwu* come forth from their special hut, instilling awe and fright among the women and children of the village. Arranging themselves on stools in order of seniority, entirely covered in raffia, with carved and painted masks where faces should be, the "dead fathers of the clan" hear and settle disputes among the villagers.

Many functions in life were accompanied by rituals and sacrifices. Three major rituals were associated with the stages of the yam-growing cycle, for example, including a major thanksgiving festival associated with the yam harvest. Nearly all Igbo were farmers, cultivating several types of yam and harvesting oil from the oil palm trees of the region. It is not surprising, therefore, that rituals and ceremonies were closely related to their farming activities. *Things Fall Apart* again provides a description of the importance of the New Yam Festival, which was in many ways a new year celebration, initiating a season of plenty and new beginnings. Feasting, dancing and drumming, and highly popular wrestling matches were enjoyed during the festival.

Oracles were also important among the Igbo, serving to establish links among Igbo communities over wide geographical areas. The oracle in a particular region had a judicial function in serving as a court of appeals or of last resort in criminal cases, offenses against the gods, or disputes among individuals. The most famous of these oracles was the *ibini okpabe* of the *Aro Chukwu* Igbo. The Aro were originally a village group of about nine villages (later nineteen) which had traders throughout Igboland. The Aro also served as agents of their oracle, investigating cases that were referred to it. There were also specialists associated with the spiritual wellbeing of the

Igbo communities. Rainmakers were also important specialists, passing on their special skill from father to son through the generations.

Most Igbo in the villages were considered to be freeborn, full citizens of the community. Persons of less than full citizen status were called *ohu*; these included slaves and "pawns" (individuals who were indentured for a specified period of time for debt payment or other obligation but who were not considered slaves). The *ohu* could eventually be absorbed into the lineage of the compound to which they were attached and their origins forgotten. Such was not the case with the very specialized group known as *osu*, descendants of persons who had been dedicated for service to a deity. *Osu* could never be absorbed into normal kinship patterns. In Chinua Achebe's novel, *No Longer at Ease*, a sequel to *Things Fall Apart*, Okonkwo's grandson, Obi, falls in love with a woman who, he later learns, is *osu*. Even Obi's parents, who are now Christians, reject the possibility that he could even consider marriage to such a person.

Although we think of the Igbo as living in independent, small-scale societies, links connected Igbo to one another. Titled societies with special initiation fees and ceremonies provided for pan-Igbo associations. Membership in such societies conferred coveted status on the title-takers. The oracles and their agents provided another kind of linkage, as did associations of diviners, found throughout the homeland of the Igbo.

Until colonial times, there was almost no history of warfare except small-scale affairs pitting one village or village-group against another. The tiny states had no standing armies, of course. Every man stood ready to arm himself and go out and fight a battle for his village as the need arose and then return to his farming. Occasionally, groups of hot-headed or restless young men would feature themselves as "warriors" or even "head-hunters," but they were not widely accepted. In the border areas of Igboland, however, martial traditions were usually stronger. In the southern border region, the Aro village-group, or clan, began to use the power of their famous oracle to collect slaves from among the other Igbo villages. The Aro took advantage of warrior classes of so-called "headhunters" that had developed most notably among the village-groups of *Abam* and *Ohafia* to serve as their military guards and mercenaries in the furtherance of Aro slave-trading activities. The particularly fierce reputations of the Abam and Ohafia are remembered still today.

The Igbo are a huge, ancient group of people located mainly in Southeastern Nigeria. Despite their dense population they did not, for the most part, develop large, centralized states; each village or small village-group was sovereign and independent. Their experience thus contrasts with that of the very closely-related Edo people who formed the powerful kingdom of Benin just to the west of the Igbo. For the most part, the Igbo in their heartland remained somewhat isolated from the effects of international trade and political upheavals until fairly recent times. On the fringes of this heartland, however, among the Igbo living west of the Niger or the peoples like the Aro or Ohafia, these external forces had more impact. The Aro, with their Ohafia and Abam allies, became very much involved in the Atlantic slave trade.

Summary

This brief summary of these three traditional societies of Nigeria reveals that they have not been static or unchanging. Many of the traditions of the Hausa have been integrated into the larger tradition of Islam. The Yoruba and Igbo also exhibit complex world views worked out over a long period of time dealing with internal changes as well as external forces represented by trade and aggressive neighbors. These people all were predominantly dependent upon agriculture—grain in the north and root crops, especially the yam, in the south. International forces and trade had more impact on the northern, Hausa peoples at first, but the reorientation of the trade, resulting from the extension of the Sudanic system toward the south and the appearance of European traders at the Coast, were to have important repercussions for the Igbo and Yoruba, as well. The rate of change accelerated with the coming of Europeans to the West African coastal region. In following chapters we will see that the Atlantic slave trade, the ending of the slave trade, and the European imposition of colonial rule over Nigeria resulted in changes more violent and sudden than those of the prior centuries.

References

1. Victor Uchendu, *The Igbo of Southeast Nigeria*, New York: Holt, Rinehart, and Winston, 1965, p. 12.
2. Luigi M. Solivetti, "Family, Marriage and Divorce in a Hausa Community: A Sociological Model," *Africa* 64 (1994), 252–253.
3. Solvetti, 256.
4. Richard E. Weekes, *Muslim Peoples: A World Ethnographic Survey*, 2nd ed. Westport, CT: Greenwood Press, 1984, p. 257.
5. Don C. Ohandike, *Anioma: A Social History of the Western Igbo People*, Athens, OH: Ohio University Press, 1994, pp. 27–32.

CHAPTER FOUR

The Coming of Colonial Nigeria: The Nineteenth Century

People throughout the African continent began to experience significant changes in their lives in the nineteenth century as a result of increasing contact with Europeans, who had until this century mainly confined their activities to the coast. By the end of the century, European states had carved up nearly the entire continent among themselves, initiating the colonial period in Africa. Even before European power reached into the interior, many parts of Africa suffered various destabilizing wars and internal migrations.

In West Africa, the main precursors of change were the effects of the Atlantic slave trade and its suppression by the British and the internal political changes wrought by a series of Islamic holy wars, or jihads, in the interior. This chapter discusses these two phenomena in turn. We begin first with some historical background concerning the Atlantic slave trade before turning to the effects of its abolition in the 1800s.

European Trade at the Coast—Development of the Slave Trade

The Portuguese began working their way gradually down the west coast of Africa under the energetic guidance of Prince Henry the Navigator. Beginning in 1415, Prince Henry sent out expedition after expedition, hoping to find a route around Africa to the rich trade of the East.

In 1481, the Portuguese founded a major post on the Gold Coast (modern Ghana), *Sao Jorge de Mina* (Elmina Castle), to trade for the gold from the interior. By 1482, they had made contact with Benin and had reached the mouth of the Congo River. Bartolomeo Dias rounded the Cape of Good Hope (then called by the Europeans the Cape of Storms) and sailed into the Indian Ocean in 1487–1488. Later expeditions, beginning with that of Vasco da Gama, took them on into the world of the Indian Ocean where they established a maritime empire stretching from Goa in India, to Malacca in the East Indies, and to Mombasa in East Africa.

View from Slave Dungeon in Elmina Castle

Along the West African coast, the Portuguese set up permanent establishments. Ambassadors were exchanged with Benin, and efforts were made to Christianize the vast empire of the Mani-Kongo inland from the mouth of the Congo River.

Early on, the Portuguese discovered the value of trading in African slaves taken from the West African coast. Minor on-shore slave raids took place as early as 1441 and 1443. Trade soon replaced raids as the standard method for obtaining the slaves. For example, the Portuguese became involved in trading horses and firearms to feuding branches of the Wolof (in modern Senegal) in return for war captives as early as 1448. The Island of Sao Tome, just south of Nigeria in the Atlantic, became an important sugar producing colony for the Portuguese, who began to import large numbers of slaves from Benin and the region around the mouth of the Congo River.

Soon the larger sea powers of Europe, Holland, England, and France, became involved. At first, these newcomers sought mainly items such as gold (an English coin became known as a *Guinea,* from the name of the region from which the gold came in West Africa), ivory, pepper, and palm oil. The discoveries in the New World, however, increased the demand for cheap labor, first for the mines of Central and South America and then for the sugar-plantations on the Caribbean islands. The Spanish crown took over the licensing of shipments of slaves to the Spanish colonies in the Americas, and this became a major source of revenue for the Spanish government. Eventually the English obtained this franchise and became the largest carrier of African slaves to the Americas.

The Dutch succeeded in taking over many of the richest parts of the far-flung Portuguese empire in the 1600s (taking Elmina in 1637, for example). The English, French, Dutch, and even Danes all acquired sugar producing West Indian colonies also in the 1600s, leading to a further increase in the demand for slave labor. Thus, European economic exploitation of Africa inaugurated a process of change in traditional Africa, the effects of which are felt even today. It is the traditional organization of African societies and the changes brought about by European intervention to which we now turn our attention.

In descriptions of Hausa, Yoruba, and Igbo cultures, we have noted the existence of various categories of people, including a traditional servile or slave status. These traditional states of slavery were normally quite different from the chattel slavery that became the basis of the long-distance slave trade of the Europeans or Arabs. A wide range of human relationships was possible in what can be termed "rights-in-persons," meaning that some people had rights over the labor and lives of others. In a simple case, a husband could expect wives to provide labor for the family farm, and fathers had similar rights over the labor of children. In other cases, individuals could hire themselves or dependents out to secure or pay off a debt. "Strangers" (those outside the local kinship system) often found themselves in similar dependent situations. Prisoners acquired in wars or sent as tribute could fall into such dependency. A group (village, lineage, family compound) or an individual might have the right of disposing of "strangers" by selling or trading them to others.

Under what circumstances could these "acquired strangers" become defined as "slaves" in the usual Western sense? This question is difficult to answer. Some dependent people eventually could become integrated into the kinship group of the "masters," losing their slave status. Once emancipated, they might acquire property, including other people who could be considered slaves. Status in society could vary, as well. Some "acquired strangers," or slaves, filled important roles in government and administration. Others—the *Osu* slaves of Igbo tradition, for example—could never change their status. European operations at the coast created a sudden huge demand for people who, in one way or another, had fallen into one of these "slave" categories. As the demand grew, so did practices such as slave-raiding and warfare to acquire prisoners, a process which destabilized African traditions and, as we shall see, in many cases the social and economic fabric of West African society.

The demographic effects of the slave trade on Africa are difficult to assess accurately. Many slave-traders kept poor records, and we can make only rough estimates about how many slaves were transported across the Atlantic or the Sahara. There is no way of knowing how many people were killed in raids and wars to acquire slaves, nor the extent of crop destruction and subsequent famine. Scholars estimate that nearly twelve million people were transported as slaves from Africa toward the Americas between 1450 and 1900. About 50 percent of these people were sent from Africa during the 1700s and nearly 30 percent during the nineteenth century.[1] The greatest period of demand coincided with the greatest expansion of the sugarcane industry from Brazil north through the Caribbean. The social and political effects of the slave trade were of great significance, and we now turn to those issues.

Impact of the Slave Trade

These effects were experienced unevenly by different African societies. Losses to specific groups varied according to location, political organization, and other factors. A marked preference for young, adult males meant that potential farmers, fathers, and warriors were lost in large numbers by some peoples. The abduction of so many men of similar age brought about tremendous imbalance and disruption in African communities which were organized along traditional gender divisions.

Throughout Africa, states arose that depended directly or indirectly on the slave trade. Although it may oversimplify some of the complexities of specific cases, one can think of an exchange of firearms for human beings as the engine driving the system. Centralized states near the coast found that they were in a position to acquire guns with which to demand tribute (payable in slaves) or to make war on neighbors. To protect themselves, some of these neighbors found it expedient to get involved in this trade in order to get the military hardware necessary for their own defense. Thus, the European demand for slave labor at once exacerbated warfare and increased its destructive capability.

In the Niger Delta, the local "People of the Salt Water" controlled access to the inland water routes. Important cities controlling outlets to the Niger and Cross Rivers became dependent on the wealth of the slave trade: these towns included Bonny (Ibani), New Calabar and Old Calabar (Kalabari), Cross Town, Duke Town, and others. The trading houses of the cities served as intermediaries, collecting slaves from the interior (from among the Igbo, usually) and trading them to British, Dutch, and other European slavers stationed in ships anchored off the coast. These towns fell under the rule of the trading houses which became, in effect, merchant oligarchies. These houses dealt through the important Igbo oracle of the Aro-Chukwu (known to Europeans as the "Long Juju"), as described in the previous chapter. Because the Aro-Chukwu oracle served as a court of last resort for the Igbo and because captured slaves were used as a kind of human currency, the oracle's fines were frequently "paid" in slaves, who were then sold to one of the coastal trading houses. In the last chapter, we saw that as the Aro slave trade became more highly organized, they resorted more frequently to the use of warrior groups from the Igbo villages of Ohafia, Abam, and others.

West of the Niger Delta, the Empire of Benin was an early source of slaves for the Portuguese sugar plantations on Sao Tome, but after dynastic wars ended and the expansion of the empire slowed in the seventeenth century, its role declined. Pepper, ivory, and cloth were still traded to the Europeans, however. Following 1700, new wars involving Benin led to the sale of war captives in return for the importation of firearms. Benin became increasingly dependent on this guns-for-slaves trade on into the nineteenth century, leading to a decline in the prosperity and power of the state.

North and west of Benin, the Yoruba Empire of Oyo grew in the 1700s as a result of slave labor on royal farms. These slaves were acquired by warfare and from trade with the north (the Sudanic trading network). The wars "produced" more captives than were needed for Oyo's internal use, though, and many were sent to the coast for sale to the Europeans in return for firearms, cloth, and cowrie shells (used as currency). The royal establishment became over-dependent on this trade, and after 1780, when the demand for slaves at the coast declined during the Napoleonic Wars, this state also went into decline.

Strife between the kings of Oyo and the increasingly powerful head of the council of elders weakened the state in the closing stages of the eighteenth century, as we have seen. Wars broke out among the other Yoruba states and Oyo. Dahomey, formerly a dependency of Oyo and much involved in the slave trade after the 1720s, warred incessantly with Oyo and other neighbors in an effort to expand its power as an independent empire. All these events served to further undermine the power and stability of Oyo.

In northern Nigeria, the Hausa states looked toward the north and the trans-Saharan trade rather than toward the south and the Atlantic slave trade. Zaria, in the southern part of Hausaland, was the city-state traditionally most involved in the slave trade. This state provided the other Hausa states with many of the slaves used for internal farming and for shipment across the Sahara to Arabic countries of North Africa. Kanem-Bornu, far from the gold sources that had fueled the trading empires of the Sudanic Kingdoms to the west, was always more dependent on the trans-Saharan slave trade than the other Sudanic empires.

By roughly the year 1800, a vast and long-standing trading network based largely on slaves in many locations had developed along the coast of West Africa, affecting states and people far into the interior. This established economy and working relationship between and among Africans and Europeans were about to be upset in the new century by a concerted effort to abolish the hated slave trade and replace it with a new economic base and a new relationship, eventually a colonial relationship, between Africans and Europeans.

The Ending of the Slave Trade

The huge expansion of the sugar industry, which correlated with the largest volume of the Atlantic slave trade, led to over-production and falling prices by the end of the eighteenth century. In England, especially, investment in new manufacturing enterprises which were not dependent on imported slave labor began to appear more attractive. In these circumstances, humanitarian movements for the abolition of the slave trade and eventually of slavery could receive a hearing in an England embarking on the "Industrial Revolution." An organized British anti-slavery campaign began around 1765 initiated by Evangelicals and Quakers. Rescued former African slaves like the famous *Olaudah Equiano*, himself an Igbo, also took part in publicizing this campaign.

Abolition, however, was a long, drawn-out process. First slavery was outlawed in England itself; then the trade in slaves was ended; finally, slavery was abolished throughout the British Empire and in other nations. The first stage was successfully concluded as early as 1772 with the *Mansfield Decision*. British abolitionists had rescued a slave from an American who had taken the slave to England. When the American regained his "property," the abolitionists brought a writ of *habeas corpus* to secure the slave's release. The Chief Justice, Lord Mansfield, held that slavery was in itself "odious," or hateful, on its face and therefore needed a law specifically legalizing it rather than a law making it specifically illegal. Since there was no such law, all slaves who touched English soil (in England itself; not elsewhere in the British Empire) were immediately and automatically freed.

Both the Mansfield Decision and the American Revolutionary War, which resulted in many slaves fleeing from the new United States into Canada, led to a growing population of freed African slaves in London and Canada. The British antislavery leader, Granville Sharp reportedly first came up with the idea of "repatriation," sending the freed slaves to a settlement in West Africa. In 1787, an expedition with 400 or 450 freed slaves was sent from London to the area of *Sierra Leone* in West Africa, where the abolitionists hoped to acquire land for a settlement. Many of these freed slaves were several generations removed from their ancestors' deportation from Africa and very few, of course, would have come from the Sierra Leone area. After difficulties with the local people, which led to the near-extinction of the colony, a large immigration of 1792 from Nova Scotia and in 1800 from Jamaica led to a firmer foundation at the settlement called Freetown.

A joint stock company was organized to help finance the new settlement. The Church Missionary Society (CMS), founded by William Wilberforce in 1799, was also an important force in supporting this experiment in repatriation. In 1808, Sierra Leone became a Crown Colony, which meant that the British government took responsibility for protecting and maintaining the settlement. This colony was to have an important effect along the West African coast and was to become important in the later history of Nigeria. In *A History of the African People*, Robert July explains: "The rise in the Freetown area of a Christian community of African repatriates, learning English and gradually becoming Europeanized, was a development of great consequence and a cast a long shadow."[2] A large proportion of freed slaves brought to Freetown in the nineteenth century were Yoruba, because the Yoruba civil wars following the breakup of the Oyo Empire provided large numbers of war captives for the trade.

The other famous experiment in the repatriation of freed slaves was in Liberia where Americans established a settlement of freed slaves at Monrovia (during the Presidency of James Monroe, in 1822). The U.S. was always ambiguous about its relationship with Liberia and never officially claimed it as a colony. The first black governor was not installed until 1841. After the European powers insisted on knowing the status of this settlement, Liberia formally declared its independence in 1847. The United States, however, did not recognize that independence until 1862 (during the American Civil War).

Meanwhile, the campaign against the slave trade continued, with Great Britain in the forefront. In 1807, an act of Parliament made it illegal for British subjects to engage in the trade. The following year, 1808, was the year the United States had set for its own abolition of the trade (but not slavery itself) as a result of the compromises at the Constitutional Convention of 1787. The tiny country of Denmark outlawed its own trade in 1803, and other European countries followed suit over the next several years. Still, the British were the most stringent in enforcing the anti-slave trade laws. They established a permanent naval force in West African waters to enforce the ban. As a result of reciprocal treaties with several other nations, the patrol gained the authority to stop and search the ships of several nations to stop the trade. The effectiveness of this effort remains unclear.

Well over a million slaves apparently were landed in the Americas between 1825 and 1865, marking the end of the American Civil War.

The British abolitionists hoped to supplement the naval interdiction with a policy of providing economic alternatives for African societies dependent on the slave trade. This policy was based on spreading Christianity, commerce, and colonization. Both the policy of suppression and the policy of ending African dependence on the trade meant increasing British involvement in local affairs along the West African coast.

The Creoles (as the freed repatriates were called) from Sierre Leone joined in the struggle against the slave trade. A college was established, the famous *Fourah Bay College*, in Sierre Leone in 1827 to train Africans to participate in missionary efforts along the coast. The first student was *Samuel Ajayi Crowther*, a Yoruba youth who been repatriated to Freetown in 1822. He went on to seminary in Britain and was later posted to a CMS missionary station in Abeokuta among the Yoruba in 1845. In 1864, Crowther became the bishop in charge of administering several CMS mission stations in Nigeria. In this role, he began to formulate ideas for African independent states on a European model, as we shall see in Chapter Six. A second generation Sierre Leonian, James Africanus Beale Horton, further systematized such thinking about modern African nationalism. Born in 1835 of Igbo parents, he was educated at Fourah Bay College and in Edinburgy, Scotland, where he received his M.D. He became a medical officer in the British army, returned to West Africa in 1859, and wrote extensively on tropical medicine and African politics.

By the middle of the nineteenth century cities were developing along the coast with an orientation that could be described as Western or European, such as St. Louis in Senegal, Monrovia in Liberia, Accra and Cape Coast in the Gold Coast (now Ghana), Lagos in Nigeria, and of course Freetown. Such westernization did not develop because of a conscious policy in London or Paris, but because of the effects of growing commercial and political involvement as the British tried to inculcate new legitimate forms of commerce to replace slave trading.

The case of the Niger Delta is a good example of how this European involvement at the cast developed. The area known to the British as the Oil Rivers, because they at first did not realize the "rivers" were really streams of the Niger Delta. Palm oil had become very important as a lubricant for machinery in the new industrial age, since petroleum oil was not yet available for this purpose.

The British appointed a consul for the Oil Rivers area in 1849, who became involved in disputes with the various delta cities over the slave trade. In 1854, the use of quinine to avoid malaria came into use, allowing European traders in steam ships to begin penetrating up the Niger River, bypassing the trading houses of coastal towns such as Bonny and Calabar.

In 1879, the very successful trading company of Sir George Goldie Taubman was inaugurated and quickly established a near monopoly on trade on the lower Niger. This company began to fulfill quasi-governmental roles along the river, especially after its designation as a company with a royal charter. Still, no official protectorate was extended over the Oil Rivers by the British until 1885, when other European powers, especially Germany and France, suddenly began to proclaim official protectorates over areas of Africa in the vicinity of Nigeria. In these circumstances, to forestall French and German ambitions in the region, Goldie's company gained its charter as the Royal Niger Company.

The resistance of some of the more centralized states against the growing European presence at the coast of West Africa also led to direct British and French control of parts of the coast. For example, in 1872 the Dutch turned over to the British the fort at Elmina Castle, an action which led to British conflict with the Ashanti Empire (which claimed ownership over the coastal area). The ensuing British-Ashanti War of 1873–1874 resulted in a British proclaiming a protectorate over the coastal area in 1874. Ironically,

Cape Coast Castle

this protectorate forestalled the efforts of Africanus Horton to develop a constitution for an independent Fanti state in the same area.

In Nigeria a similar process resulted in a British colony at Lagos in southwestern Nigeria. In 1851, the British consul from the Oil Rivers, with British military support, replaced one reigning king of Lagos with another. The British hoped that the new king would be more cooperative in helping to prevent slave trading. The British at Lagos then found themselves embroiled in internal wars among the Yoruba in the hinterland, leading to the establishment of an official British colony at Lagos in 1861. Continued strife with the Egba branch of the Yoruba ultimately resulted in the expulsion of the CMS mission station at Abeokuta, the one originally set up by Crowther. In this way, the British become more and more involved in the affairs in the hinterland.

The ending of the slave trade and the extension of new commercial ventures by the British in the Nigeria area resulted in the gradual extension of British official involvement all along the coast of Nigeria. This involvement rapidly accelerated during the period of the so-called "Scramble for Africa" by the Europeans in the last fifteen years of the century. The "Scramble," which initiates the colonial period, is further described in the following chapter. We now turn our attention to the second of the major events that began the reorganization of political life in the interior regions of Nigeria.

The Fulani Jihads

While the people of southern Nigeria were experiencing the profound changes associated with the ending of the slave trade, the Hausa in the north experienced a revolutionary upheaval and reorganization of their own. A powerful centralized state united the Hausa kingdoms in a new Islamic empire under the rule of the Fulani. Recall that the pastoral Fulani are found throughout the West African Sudan. Two branches had developed: the nomadic herding peoples of the rural countryside and the Islamized town Fulani.

These town Fulani provided the leadership for a series of Islamic uprisings resulting in the establishment of Islamic states throughout West Africa. Beginning in the western part of the Sudanic corridor in the 1700s, Fulani imams became rulers of small Islamic theocratic states. They came to power by overthrowing traditional leaders who did not seem to the Fulani clerics to be strict enough in their observances of Islamic law and practice. These jihads became part of the tradition of the Fulani, influencing important jihadists of the nineteenth century, of whom the most famous of all was *Uthman dan Fodio* in northern Nigeria. The jihad that shook Nigeria, therefore, should be seen as part of a movement widespread in West Africa.

The leaders of these major jihads were members of important Sudanic sufi orders and brotherhoods). Uthman dan Fodio, for example, was a member of the *Qadiriyya* brotherhood. The followers of these brotherhoods believed that the thirteenth century after the *hegira* (the date in 622 when the Prophet Muhammed emigrated from Mecca to Medina) would be a millennial age. Many Muslims in West Africa expected a leader to arise as the twelfth in a line of great jihad leaders to renew the struggle for the purification of Islam. Some believed that *Askia* Muhammed of Songhai had been the eleventh of these anticipated reformers. Uthman dan Fodio, as well as other great jihad leaders in West Africa of the nineteenth century, claimed to be on a mission to restore the purity of Islamic society among the faithful in West Africa. Uthman dan Fodio testified to a mystical vision he had experienced in 1794 in which Muhammed the Prophet commissioned him to "unsheathe the Sword of Truth" against the enemies of Islam in West Africa.

Throughout the Islamized area of West Africa, the Sudanic savannas in which the great trading empires had risen and fallen, there had long been tension between the orthodox Muslim leaders and the traditional rulers, who professed Islam but permitted traditional practices to continue to maintain their legitimacy with the people. At an earlier time, we observed how this tension led to instability in the Mali and Songhai states, as in the overthrow of *Sunni* Ali's dynasty of Songhai by *Askia* Muhammed the Great. The early eighteenth century jihads in the far Western region of the Sudanic corridor similarly resulted from this tension between the devout and those seen as pragmatic compromisers. By the end of the eighteenth century the Hausa states, in which the rulers had grown corrupt and remote from the common people, were ripe for Islamic revolution.

Uthman dan Fodio, born in 1754 in the northern Hausa state of Gobir, began teaching around age 20. His family consisted of distinguished scholars and teachers and inclined toward Muslim reform. The ruler of Gobir became suspicious of dan Fodio's preaching against misgovernment, and there may have been an attempt on Uthman dan Fodio's life around 1789. During the 1790s his preaching grew more militant, leading to the ruler's edict that none of dan Fodio's followers would be allowed to teach or preach in Gobir (dan Fodio himself seems to have been too powerful to suffer this restriction).

The veneration that people had for Uthman dan Fodio is revealed in a series of miracle stories told about him. For example, a Hausa caravan leader capsized his canoe full of kola nuts while crossing the Niger. He called upon the great *Shehu* (a title of Uthman dan Fodio) to save him, promising a gift of ten calabashes (large gourds used as baskets) full of kolas. At that exact point in time, the *Shehu* was preaching in Sokoto; he paused to wring water out of the sleeve of his garment and continued preaching. At the same time, the merchant felt a powerful hand lift his boat from raging waters to safety. Upon arriving at Sokoto several days later, the trader found Uthman dan Fodio and offered him three calabashes of kolas in gratitude for his rescue. The *Shehu* gently reminded him, however, that he had promised ten calabashes.[3] The story not only reveals a belief in Uthman dan Fodio's power, but also emphasizes the importance of the kola trade to the Hausa.

A new king, said to have been a student of dan Fodio's, openly attacked him upon coming to power in 1802. Uthman dan Fodio proclaimed a jihad in 1804 against the Hausa rulers, turning military command over to his son, Muhammed Bello. By 1808, the capital of Gobir, the city of Alkalawa, had fallen to the Fulani jihadists. The Fulani flocked to his banner and by 1811 all of Hausaland was under control of forces loyal to the great *Shehu*. The jihad in areas outside Gobir, in Kano, Zaria, or Borno for instance, were carried on by Fulani clan leaders, recognized as "flag-bearers" for Uthman dan Fodio. These leaders, when successful, became his *Emirs*, or deputies, in newly established territories. After Uthman dan Fodio retired from active service in 1812, Uthman's son, Muhammed Bello, became the Caliph of the empire based on the new center of Sokoto. The rulers of the Hausa states were replaced by the emirs, who were subordinate to the Caliph of Sokoto.

The Fulani forces also pushed on beyond the Hausa states, attacking the Junkun state in the region of the Benue, moving toward the state of Kanem-Borno to the north and east, and toward the Yoruba state of Oyo to the south. New emirates continued to be carved out of these and other areas.

Throughout the realms of the Oyo Empire, thousands of Hausa and Fulani slaves revolted and fled to the northern Yoruba city of Ilorin. Fighting between the traditional ruler of Oyo and Muslim-led rebels ultimately led to a Muslim victory. The son of a Muslim *mallam* became the new ruler, or emir, and gave his allegiance to the Empire of Sokoto in the North. Ilorin thus broke away from the Empire of Oyo, beginning the disintegration of the largest Yoruba state and a period of great instability and warfare among the Yoruba.

Kanem-Borno, now usually referred to simply as Borno, had lost much of its earlier strength. Still, some of the Hausa states such as Kano and Katsina owed tribute to the *Mais*; for that reason, the rulers of Kano and Daura called on the *Mai* of Borno for assistance against the jihad launched by Uthman dan Fodio. Such assistance was defeated easily as Kano fell to the Fulani, encouraging some of the Fulani to carry the attack into Borno itself. Some small emirates were established in areas formerly part of Borno and even the capital was captured in 1808. The *Mai* turned for help to another remarkable Islamic leader, a Muslim scholar and leader of the pastoral Kanembu people, *al-Kanemi*. This new leader took on Muhammed Bello's forces in argument as well as in battle, and managed to retake most of the Borno state. Although al-Kanemi was the real power in the state, he did leave the *Mai* on the throne. He instituted changes making Borno a Muslim theocracy.

Meanwhile, the new Empire of Sokoto reorganized the entire area of Hausaland. At first, many disputes arose among various military commanders and Muslim scholars trying to administer the newly-won, widespread territories. When *Shehu* Uthman dan Fodio retired to teach and write in 1812, judging these disputes was divided between his brother Abdullahi, installed as the Emir of Gwandu, and Muhammed Bello. Uthman dan Fodio fell ill in 1815 and died in 1817, at which point his son, Muhammed Bello, succeeded to the office of Caliph. After their conquest of the area, the British renamed the Caliph as the Sultan, a somewhat lesser title.

By 1820, the Caliphate of Sokoto comprised seven major emirates, with ten more in the process of being formed. The emirs were selected on the basis of Muslim piety as well as on their original leadership in the jihad. There were two centers of power in the empire: at Gwandu and at Sokoto. While the Caliph, now Muhammed Bello, was the political leader of the state, the Emir of Gwandu was respected for piety and religious leadership. Some of the western emirates were administered from Gwandu, but the larger and more important eastern emirates, such as Kano and Katsina, were subordinate directly to Sokoto.

This system depended upon the personal relationship between the Caliph and the Emir of Gwandu, and their relationships with the individual emirs. In practice, these relationships among old comrades-in-arms and fellow students seemed to work very well. Muhammed Bello's uncle did not appear to have ambitions to challenge the caliph for supremacy. Most emirs exercised significant independent authority within their realms. During the middle part of the nineteenth century, despite some continued raids and campaigns, the caliphate remained a region of relative peace and prosperity. The empire provided the framework which allowed the British to apply their famous "indirect rule" during their colonial reign.

Summary

The nineteenth century was thus a time of upheaval and change as all the regions of West Africa, except Liberia, moved toward colonial status to follow the subsequent European conquests at the end of the century. The West African slave trade had developed over a period of several previous centuries and directly involved many coastal peoples and states, including those in Nigeria. Benin and Oyo, especially through its subordinate state of Dahomey, were at times much involved in this trade as were the small trading city-states south of the Igbo homeland in Eastern Nigeria. The British efforts at suppressing the slave trade led to their own increasing presence along the coast, especially following the establishment of the freed-slave colony of Sierre Leone. This presence led to increasing British involvement in internal affairs of various African states.

European influence began to penetrate Africa during the nineteenth century. The growing presence of the British along the West African coast was especially notable. This period also saw the expansion of the Empire of Sokoto. Throughout much of the African continent, this century was a period of growing insecurity and destabilization.

Also in this century people in the interior, savanna regions of Northern Nigeria experienced the great Fulani jihads, launched by the outstanding Muslim leader and scholar, Uthman dan Fodio. As a result of this series of jihads, a theocratic Muslim empire ruled over by people now referred to as Hausa-Fulani, dominated much of the area of modern-day Northern Nigeria.

By the beginning of the colonial period at the end of the century, the area of modern Nigeria was divided between a Muslim North and an increasingly unstable South, rent by the Yoruba wars in the Southwest, the decline of the slave trading city-states of the Niger Delta and coast, and new and destabilizing influences from traders and missionaries in the Igbo heartland. A new group of Africans with Western-style education and cultural affinities, many of them descendants of slaves freed as a result of the British anti-slavery patrols, had appeared along the coast from Sierre Leone to Lagos, southern Yorubaland, and the Niger Delta region.

References

1. Catherine Coquery-Vidrovitch, *Africa: Endurance and Change South of the Sahara*, trans. David Maisel. Los Angeles: UCLA Press, 1988, pp.19–20.

2. Robert W. July, *A History of the African People*, New York: Charles Scribners, 1970, p. 271.

3. Mervyn Hiskett, *The Development of Islam in West Africa*, London and New York: Longman, 1984, pp. 130–131.

CHAPTER FIVE

The Colonial Period in Nigeria

The occupation of Africa by the European nations not only happened quickly, it happened out of the sight of most of the world. There was no CNN or any kind of mass media to broadcast these events to an international audience. To people outside Africa the conquest of the African peoples was not something that attracted a lot of attention at the time. As a result, a rather common view developed in Europe and America that the occupation was relatively peaceful and even welcomed by the inhabitants of African lands. The actual picture was more complicated, as we shall see in the opening parts of this chapter. And, the colonial system imposed on the peoples of Africa, particularly Nigeria, had mixed results.

While European influence continued to grow along the coasts of Africa during the 1800s, most of the African continent remained independent well into the 1880s. Here and there European states had established imperial control over relatively small areas. The British had taken over the former Dutch-controlled South African Cape, causing some of the Dutch settlers to retreat further into the interior of southern Africa. The French had established a colony in the area of Senegal and were beginning to push up the Senegal River into the western Sudan. Such cases represented exceptions, however, as for the most part there were only scattered posts, like the British colony at Lagos, or Cape Coast in modern-day Ghana, or the freed-slave colony at Freetown in Sierre Leone.

The Scramble for Africa

Suddenly in about the last fifteen years of the century, European nations carved up nearly the entire continent among themselves. By the start of the twentieth century, the map of Africa was painted in the red of Great Britain, the green of France, and other imperial colors. Where there had been no European presence, there was a Belgian Congo, French West Africa, German East Africa, and so on. Only the Empire of Ethiopia in the northeast and the Republic of Liberia in the west retained their independence. The acquisition of all this colonial territory went so quickly that observers called it a land scramble—the "Scramble for Africa."

The most important of many factors leading to this scramble was the international rivalry among the powers of Europe. The territories of Africa were seized not for their own sake but to forestall the claims of other European

nations. Of course there were hopes that some of the colonies would provide minerals or other products valuable to the imperial powers, but material interests of this sort were often a secondary consideration.

What factors lay behind the urge for empire in nineteenth century Europe?
Germany and Italy became unified states for the first time in history and
began to compete for resources in Africa and Asia, as well as for international respect and power. An energetic new King of the Belgians, Leopold
II, looked to a colonial empire as a quick way to enhance the prosperity and
prestige of his small nation. France, following her defeat by the newly unified Germany in a brief war in 1870 and smarting under Britain's dominance over the Suez Canal, became aggressive in pushing for empire. All
these powers carried their ambitions and rivalries into the African arena.

King Leopold hired the famous explorer, Henry Morton Stanley, to make
treaties with African rulers along the Congo River and to develop a land
and water transport system in the Congo Basin. French officers began sign-
ing treaties with Africans north of the Congo River in competition with
Leopold's agents. Meanwhile, in the delta and lower stretches of the Niger
River, a British trader named George Goldie Taubman (who usually went
by the name of Goldie) organized all the other British traders into a monopoly, driving out competition, and further extending British influence in
southern Nigeria.

Matters came to a head in 1883–1884 when the leader of the new German
Empire, Chancellor Bismarck, became involved and suddenly declared
German protectorates over far-flung parts of the African continent. Bismarck probably meant to use his African acquisitions as leverage to gain
influence in European politics. The British could not fail to notice that each
new German dependency was adjacent to an area of strategically important British territory—in East Africa, South Africa, and West Africa. For
example, the Germans proclaimed a protectorate over Togoland, right next
to the British sphere along the Gold Coast (now Ghana), and over the area
of Cameroon (Kamerun being the German name for the area), next door to
the Niger Delta region, long a British sphere of influence, as we have seen.

With the Belgians claiming the middle of the continent, the French forcing
their way up the rivers into the western Sudan, and the Germans pushing
north toward Lake Chad and the old empire of Kanem-Borno, the race was
on. The Portuguese, who had long claimed control over the mouth of the
Congo River protested the sudden entrance of Germans, French, and Belgians into that area. To avert war among the European states (but with no

effort to prevent war with African peoples), an international conference was called at Berlin for the winter of 1884–1885 to work out an "orderly" process for acquiring African territory.

The ostensible purpose of this Congress of Berlin was to set up rules allowing for free trade along the Niger and Congo Rivers. Although the final act of the conference gave lip service to free trade, the practical result was to recognize the primacy of the British on the Niger and the primacy of the newly named Congo Free State along the Congo River (the Free State was essentially a private organization under the personal control of King Leopold). Of more significance for Africans was the provision of the final agreement requiring those European powers claiming territory in Africa to guarantee they had established "effective occupation" of such territory. While by mutual agreement this requirement could be ignored or minimized, the "effective occupation" clause motivated European governments to put their people, usually soldiers and administrators, on the ground, especially in areas disputed among various European powers.

British Fortifications along West African Coast

Following the Berlin Congress, Goldie's company was granted a royal charter giving his company quasi-governmental authority in the Niger Delta in areas where his agents had signed treaties with African leaders. The use of private companies with royal charters became standard practice for the expansion of British influence. Recall that the first British colonists in America had such charters to set up colonies in Virginia, Massachusetts, and so on. The British had taken over the vast colony of India mainly through the British East Indies Company. In Africa, Cecil Rhodes organized the British South Africa Company to extend British control over much of southern Africa, including the diamond-producing areas. Now, in Nigeria, the Royal Niger Company became the mechanism for British imperialism.

British Occupation of Nigeria

The British occupation of Nigeria proceeded through four over-lapping stages between 1885 and 1910. First, they blocked French ambitions along the Lagos coastal area and extended their control over the warring Yoruba kingdoms. Second, the forces of the Royal Niger Company subdued the Fulani emirates of the north, taking of the Empire of Sokoto. Third, they continued to eliminate resistance of the Niger Delta city-states. Finally, the British embarked on a series of "pacification" campaigns to bring the Igbo hinterland under their control. The village-based societies of Igbo were the last areas to be subdued. Because of the fragmented nature of the political systems there, it was necessary to conquer this last region almost village by village. We now turn to a brief description of each of these phases.

The lands of the Yoruba people were torn by nearly continuous warfare throughout much of the nineteenth century. These wars resulted from the break-up of the old empire of Oyo and the efforts of newer Yoruba states to seize more power. As the sources of slaves and other trade were cut off—in the north by the Fulani jihads and in the south by the antislavery mission of the British, the Oyo Empire lost much of its power base. The Oyo army lost much of its effectiveness and cohesion. External factors hastening disintegration included Fulani incursions from the north and assertions of independence by the Dahomean Empire in the west. With the fall of Ilorin to the jihadists and its establishment as an emirate of the Sokoto Empire, Oyo was increasingly isolated. The armies of Oyo were defeated in a series of battles as they struggled to maintain control of their empire. Soldiers in fact became cut off from a return to Oyo, so they often became wandering bands of warriors in search of new homes. After the final defeat of Oyo by Ilorin in 1835 and the death of the reigning *Alafin* in the battle, the ancient city of Oyo was abandoned and her people migrated to the south where the forested areas provided more protection from Fulani cavalry. A new Oyo was established (the one that appears on modern maps of Nigeria) and the new powerful city-states of Ibadan and Abeokuta were established by people dislocated by these forced migrations.

As the Oyo Empire disintegrated, fighting broke out throughout Yorubaland. The British, trying to end the slave trade and provide order and protection for their traders and missionaries, were increasingly involved in the internal Yoruba affairs.

A major expedition leading to the occupation of all of Yorubaland was a British-led invasion to open roads between Lagos and an inland city of a branch of Yoruba called the Ijebu. The people and allies from the new city of Abeokuta had refused to allow trade from the coast to the city of Ibadan. In 1892 a force of 450 men, mostly Hausa and West Indians along with 100 men from Ibadan, started north from Lagos (note that the conquest was carried out mainly by African or colonial troops under the leadership of British officers—not by British troops). This force was equipped with modern rifles, cannon, one machine gun, and some rocket launchers. This small force defeated a Yoruba army of about 10,000 men, which suffered many casualties. These Yoruba quickly made peace with the British and rest of the Yoruba rulers signed treaties with the British as well. One of the leading men among the Ijebu Yoruba became British-supported and a convert to Islam. Today one of the major festivals in the Ijebu city, coinciding with an important Muslim festival, recalls parades by supporters of this early leader representing British control through indirect rule.

The British turned their attention next to the north and the Caliphate of Sokoto. The Royal Niger Company had concluded a treaty with the Caliph, which the company interpreted as giving them a protectorate over his empire. The Caliph, on the other hand, thought he had merely granted the company a monopoly over trade with Europeans in his lands. In 1897, the company invaded two of the southernmost emirates, Ilorin and Nupe, and defeated them. In 1899, the British government took over the company and all its property, withdrawing the royal charter but paying a handsome indemnity to the stockholders. The following year, the British undertook to enforce "effective occupation" of the domains of the empires of Sokoto and Kanem-Borno (now called, simply, Borno).

A notorious slave center called Kontogora was one of the first of the Fulani emirates to fall. Some important cities, such as Zaria, gave in without a fight in the face of superior British armaments. The conquest of Kano, the most important of the northern cities and key to the British strategy, required a major expedition, however, in 1902. Again, in actual numbers the British force was quite small—772 African soldiers of West African Frontier Force, or WAFF, and 36 British officers. They were equipped with machine guns and cannon, however. When they reached Kano, the cannon battered down the wall at one point, which allowed the city to be taken easily. Another Fulani force, coming from the city of Sokoto, attacked the British force, but their cavalry charges against machine guns were ineffective and devastating to the Fulani.

The British attacked Sokoto itself and defeated the army of the new Caliph, who was killed in the process. The British then appointed a new Caliph, but with the diminished title of Sultan. This new Sultan of Sokoto sided with the British when there was another uprising at the city of Sokoto in 1906. Currently, the Sultan of Sokoto is today the nominal head of Muslims in Nigeria.

The third phase of the British military occupation of Nigeria involved minor but troublesome expeditions in the area of the Niger Delta. Although the British influence in the area was fairly long-standing, in the form of the Oil Rivers Protectorate (re-named the Niger Coast Protectorate in 1893), pockets of resistance still were holding out.

The British sent one expedition against a ruler blocking access to the Benin River in 1894, and a more famous expedition against the still independent city of Benin in 1897. The expedition against Benin is particularly illustrative of the process of "effective occupation." The *Oba* of Benin refused to allow free trade through his domains. The British claimed a second cause for war was the continuation of human sacrifice at Benin. The British Consul-General was killed on a visit to Benin City in January 1897; hostilities broke out. The British expedition set out in February, and tragically the *Oba* resorted to human sacrifices throughout the city to generate ritual power to defeat the British. The city was looted of its art treasures—the famous Benin bronzes and ivory carvings now found in museums around the world—the *Oba* was deported. The leader of the British expedition, Lord Baden-Powel, later founder of the Boy Scouts, reported without irony that as the British soldiers packed up all the art treasures to take away to Britain, he said he was proud to have observed no "looting." Presumably officially stealing treasures by government action was considered to be something other than looting.

The military phase of the occupation of the interior of Igboland lasted longer than that of other areas of Nigeria—from around 1900 to as late as 1910, although some scattered opposition continued until World War I began in 1914. The British had to defeat armies of warriors piece-meal in each village and village-group. The dense forest worked to the disadvantage of the invading colonial forces as well. The British forces mounted the first major expedition in the area against the Aro-Chukwu, because of their continued involvement in slaving in the Delta region. The campaign took nearly six months in 1901 before the British were finally able to enter the central town of the Aro-Chukwu and burn the shrine and image of their famous oracle. Thus was the fourth phase of the military occupation of most of the entire area of modern-day Nigeria completed.

Following the establishment of the African colonies, Europeans and Americans accepted the idea the imposition of the colonial rule had been peaceful for the most part and sometimes even welcomed by the African peoples themselves. This brief summary of the British conquest of Nigeria shows, however, there was armed resistance. In may parts of Nigeria, as well as the rest of Africa in general, the European conquest, while small-scale by the standards of European warfare, was violent and deadly.

The Colonial System in Nigeria

The British Empire in Africa, like those of other European nations, was acquitted almost in a state of absent-mindedness. Once the colonies were secured militarily, the Europeans were often less than certain what to do with them. The first phase of colonialism, as we have seen involved the gradual extension of authority over the people and the territory. By the end of this phase the British had huge territories in eastern and southern Africa, while the French controlled vast stretches of West Africa. The British colonies in West Africa, although smaller than the French colonies, were by and large the richest in resources and the most populous.

Colonial Infrastructure and Economies

In acquiring their African colonies, the British had no intention of creating any new tax burdens on their own citizens, and so the colonies had to be inexpensive to administer and, it was hoped, self-supporting in a very short time. Direct grants from the British government were used initially to pay for "pacification," that is, the military campaigns to put down local resistance, and for the early construction of an infrastructure, like new roads and railways.

The second phase of colonialism was marked by efforts to develop economic self-sufficiency in the newly acquired colonies. Three methods were available to colonial governments in Africa:

- Cash crops. First, European administrators could induce African farmers to grow "cash crops," which were crops for sale on the international market, in place of subsistence crops for food. The sale of the crops would put money in the hands of Africans, which could then be taxed for government revenues.

- European settlers. Second, they could encourage European settlers to go out to live in the colonies and to hire Africans to work on farms or in mines for them. They could then tax the Africans' wages to pay for colonial administration.

- Concessionaire companies. Third, they could turn over to private companies the rights to exploit mineral or agricultural resources, in exchange for the private companies' financing building roads, railways, and the like.

The unifying purpose of these methods was to bring African people into a cash-based economy so that they could be taxed by colonial governments. A second purpose was to make Africans consumers of manufactured goods from the European colonial country, paid for with the new cash wages. Africa, in turn, was to export products such as palm oil, rubber, coffee, cocoa, gold, ivory, and copper for European consumption. As a result, the African colonies developed economies based on the extraction of resources, rather than local production of manufactured goods.

Even before the colonial period, a market in cash crops developed along the West African coast and in Nigeria particularly. This development, coupled with a climate unhealthy for European settlement, helped determine that cash crops grown by African farmers would be the basic method for economic development in Nigeria. The Niger Delta was already one of the leading areas in the world for the export of palm products. In Yorubaland, cocoa became the major product. In the north, the major cash crops became groundnuts (also known as peanuts) and cotton.

To facilitate the expansion and transportation of these cash crops, the colony had to build a new transportation system. Beginning from Lagos in 1898, the colonial government constructed a rail line all the way to Kano by 1912. New harbors were dredged out at Lagos and also at the new city in the east called Port Harcourt. By 1920 a second railway line extended from Port Harcourt north through Igboland and on up to Zaria, where it connected with the line to Kano. Typically in West Africa the lines of transportation and communication run north-south from the coast to the interior, with few east-west connections. Colonial governments developed communication systems suited to their own needs and interests—getting products out of the interior for export from the coast.

Indirect Rule

The British based their administration of the colony of Nigeria on the philosophy of "indirect rule" as worked out by Frederick Lugard in his years administering northern Nigeria. While indirect rule had provided a basis for some British administration of colonies such as India before, Lugard worked out the idea much more systematically as the fundamental principle of colonial administration.

As the term implies, indirect rule involves maintaining the traditional rulers of an area as functionaries ultimately answerable to the real authority of the colonial government. The emirs of northern Nigeria, already in place as subsidiary rulers or governors under the Caliph of Sokoto, provided an ideal model for this system. Lugard placed a British "resident" with each emir. The function of the resident was to advise the emir and give him instructions regarding his administration. The term, "resident," was intended to imply the British administrator was merely "in residence" with the emir, rather than a superior. If fact, the resident gave directions to the emir and his officers, who then became essentially part of the overall colonial administration. The resident was required to maintain the dignity and trappings associated with the traditional ruler. In northern Nigeria, this policy meant that Islam would be sheltered as a pillar to the traditional legitimacy of the local rulers. Christian missionaries were therefore largely excluded from operating in the north. The Caliph, now called the Sultan of Sokoto, was also left in place as spiritual head for the Hause-Fulani states of the north. Although the British political officers were supposed to help "modernize" emirate administration, in practice they saw their function as preserving the old customs and practices. As a result, indirect rule in the north has been criticized for freezing a suppressive system in place.

The system of indirect rule instituted by Lugard in the north seemed to work so well in northern Nigeria (that is, it seemed to be efficient and cost-effective for the British) that he tried to extend it throughout the colony as north and south were combined into the Colony of Nigeria. Lugard became the Governor-General overall of Nigeria, while he appointed two lieutenant-governors, one for Northern Nigeria and one for Southern Nigeria. This action led to the unfortunate result of maintaining a north-south division in the country that persists and troubles the politics of Nigeria still today.

Efforts to implement the system of indirect rule in the south were much less successful, from the British point of view, than had been the case with the northern emirates. While the system might seem practicable for a central-ized kingdom such as old Benin, it was less so among people such as the Yoruba, where the power of rulers like the *Alafin* was more limited. During the time of the First World War, for example, uprisings in parts of Yoruba-land broke out when people felt the newly appointed rulers exceeded the traditional authority of their offices.

Among small-scale political societies, such as the Igbo, the system was especially difficult to implement. The British administration decided to subdivide traditional African political units, designating some as "advanced" and others, "primitive." The so-called "primitive" areas were those which appeared to the colonial officials to be "stateless"—the small-scale, democratic societies like those of the Igbo. Critics of colonialism, in Britain and elsewhere, had to wonder at a system that terms autocratic emi-rates as advanced and democratic systems as primitive.

To implement indirect rule among the Igbo and similarly organized peo-ples, the British used a system of appointing "warrant chiefs." Likely can-didates from the elders or respected community leaders in a village or village-group were made chiefs by "warrant." These warrant chiefs then participated on a so-called Native Council, which performed executive and judicial functions in a particular area. This method of forcing indirect rule on peoples and areas where it was inappropriate is illustrated in the novel, *Arrow of God*, by Chinua Achebe. The British District Commissioner offers the novel's protagonist, Ezeulu, the warrant chieftaincy for his village. The commissioner is puzzled and irritated when Ezeulu turns down this "honor." Often in real life the position of warrant chief went to one the peo-ple known as "new men," those who prospered under the new regime but did not meet traditional criteria for leadership. Often, such "new men" were resented among the Igbo and similar peoples.

If indirect rule had clear benefits for the British administrators (it was economical, efficient, and generally effective as far as their interests were concerned), its benfits for the Africans were fewer. Although the system of indirect rule was probably less disruptive of local customs than direct foreign control might have been, there were many negative effects. The most damaging may have been the altering of internal control mechanisms of traditional societies. For example, as noted in regard to the northern emirates, indirect rule could perpetuate corrupt or autocratic rulers frozen in place during a time of profound political and economic changes in the country. Newly educated African elites, ironically, were "frozen out" by the same system, which had few political roles for newly educated lawyers, doctors, teachers, and other professionals. And, as we have seen, indirect rule ignored the political realities of small-scale societies.

Consequences of the Colonial Period

The colonial period in Nigeria, as in most of Africa, proved to be a brief but highly significant interlude. Over a period of about sixty years, the new nation of Nigeria was created where no such entity had existed before. The early stages of the colonial administration (1905–1920) saw the development of new infrastructure necessary to the development of a modern nation-state—roads, harbors, railroads, bridges.

This infrastructure was the first important element in the changes leading to a new Nigeria. In the early stages of road-building, much of the construction was done by forced-labor in the place of taxes. These roads created new markets and commercial opportunities and made it possible for the African people to travel over a much wider area than many had before. The Igbo, for example, spread from southeast Nigeria throughout the colony as traders and employees of the colonial government. In the growing new cities, many kinds of peoples from diverse ethnic backgrounds were brought together for the first time.

A second important effect of colonialism was the creation of a cash-based economy. The necessity imposed by the government for people to pay taxes in the form of currency provided the first real impetus to this system. The development of cash crops as rural and urban labor paid in currency followed. The cash economy was fueled by interest in European manufactured goods, unknown in Africa much before colonial times—bicycles, radios, and European-style clothing.

A third effect was the growth of cities and towns. Lagos became a major urban area. Kano, already a major city, tripled in size during colonial times as a new railroad terminus. New cities, such as Port Harcourt, sprang up and grew rapidly. In these new urban centers, ethnic identities took on new significance as newcomers looked for familiar ways and languages to help ease the transition into the milieu of the strange large city, which brought together people of many different backgrounds.

Table 2. Principal Nigerian Cities
Estimated Population 2006

City	Population	Dominant Ethnic Region*
Lagos (former capital)	7,182,000	Yoruba, others
Kano	2,994,000	Hausa-Fulani
Ibadan	2,537,000	Yoruba
Kaduna	1,373,000	Hausa-Fulani
Benin City	1,054,000	Edo
Port Harcourt	972,000	Ijaw, Igbo
Zaria	846,000	Hausa-Fulani
Ogbomosho	598,000	Yoruba
Enugu	563,000	Igbo
Oyo (new Oyo)	511,000	Yoruba
Abeokuta	487,000	Yoruba

*All large cities are ethnically mixed; this designation indicates the historical or regional designation of the modern city.

A fourth important effect lay in the development of an institutionalized, "Westernized" education system. Throughout southern Nigeria schools were associated with Christian missionaries so that there developed a connection between obtaining a "modern" education and converting to the new faith. Such an education had the effect of undermining the traditional bases for age groups and initiation ceremonies that had constituted much of an education in earlier times.

In politics, a fifth effect grew from the tendency of colonial administrations to undercut traditional systems of governance. It was obvious, even with indirect rule, that traditional rulers were no longer actually independent or sovereign. They were clearly taking orders from colonial administrators. A related consequence lay in the growing realization that there was some unity among Africans in general, since they were all treated similarly by the new colonial rulers. Africans became conscious of new, shared identity, and became aware they were, in fact, all Africans. The goal of the newly developing African political awareness was to win rights: first, within the colonial system, and eventually as part of an effort to take over existing colonial structures. Thus, the colonial state became the basis for future political identification.

Summary

The Euorpean "Scramble for Africa," ushered in the colonial period in West Africa. Rivalries among the European states themselves occasioned this scramble for territorial claims more than intrinsic interests in the African lands themselves. Nigeria fell to the British, bring to closure a long-developing period of growing British involvement along the Nigerian Coast and the Niger Delta. The conquest was a military occupation and not always peaceful or nonviolent, even though it was often depicted as such in popular British and American thought.

Following the rapid carving up of Africa, the European powers were unsure what to do next. Once in power, the British adopted the policy of "indirect rule" for their African colonies, on the model used by Lord Lugard in northern Nigeria. Because of Nigeria's climate and disease environment was not conducive to British settlement, the colonial officials encouraged African farmers to grow cash crops in order to earn currency which they use to pay taxes to meet the expenses of the colonial government.

The colonial period in Nigeria was relatively brief—much briefer, for example, than British occupation of many of the colonies that became the United States of America. Major changes took place over this period of 60 to 70 years, however. A new infrastructure of roads, railroads, harbors, bridges, and new waterways provided for easier movement of people and goods. This infrastructure also made it easier for the colonial powers to extract natural resources and agricultural commodities from Nigeria and the growth of new urban centers. During this period, the Igbo people in particular spread throughout the new colony, serving as shopkeepers, clerks, and in other positions created by the new colonial administration.

Especially in these new urban centers, ethnic identities became more significant and divisive than they had been before. As a result, large groups, such as the Igbo, Yoruba, and Hausa-Fulani developed a strong sense of ethnic consciousness beyond the scope of earlier times. In addition, the colonial government preferred to categorize peoples by simple, large ethic groupings to facilitate administration, and such categories took on lives of their own with consequences that we will see in the following chapters.

CHAPTER SIX

African Nationalism in Nigeria

The establishment of colonial governments in Africa was immediately followed by political movements intended to influence and eventually to end the colonial regimes. Over time, the goal of these movements came to be to replace the white colonial officials with African presidents and parliamentarians, presiding over new African nations within artificially created national borders. In Nigeria, even more so than in many other African colonies, powerful allegiances based on regionalism, religion, and newly significant ethic identifications complicated this political development.

Early Stages of African Nationalism

Nationalism, the striving for African independence, passed through several stages. The first stage, seen in the previous chapter, was resistance to the European military occupation of the country. At this stage, the goal of the African leaders was to restore a pre-existing state, empire, or village society. In the second stage, Africans, often from different ethnic backgrounds, developed notions of general grievances, cutting across these differing traditional and ethnic lines. Racial discrimination, forced labor, taxation, and general lack of African representation in their own government represented issues typical of such general grievances. The third stage saw the development of political organizations and parties often begun by a small, western-educated class among the Africans. These organizations went beyond resistance and protest looking to more of a political program for African representation in government. In the fourth stage, the political mobilization and political party formation extended from the few to the many, to the masses.

As with many social and cultural changes, African nationalism in the colonial period was preceded by various intellectual antecedents.

One of the most important antecedents shaping nationalism along the West African coast involved the Creole elites, especially those from Sierre Leone. Recall that as a result of the British anti-slavery patrols, beginning in the early 1800s, many freed slaves had been settled at Freetown in modern-day Sierre Leone. These settlers, although from many different areas along the coast, comprised a large number from Yorubaland and Igboland. We saw that the first African bishop of the Anglican Church in Nigeria was *Samuel*

Ajayi Crowther, who could be considered an early forerunner of African nationalism. Crowther became an essential participant in the effort by the Church Missionary Society (CMS) of the Anglican Church to support an independent African church led to educated Sierre Leonians along the coast. He is best known for leading the CMS mission established at Abeokuta in Yorubaland. He was also a foremost linguist, helping to translate the Bible and other religious documents into his native Yoruba.

In 1864, Crowther was installed as Anglican Bishop for the church in West Africa beyond the bounds of British dependencies. The unusual nature of his appointment (effective only outside British-controlled territory) reveals the nature of internal controversy within the British church regarding the role of Africans themselves in the leadership of the West African church. By the end of the century, the British church bureaucracy pulled back from allowing leadership to pass directly to Africans, as Crowther was replaced in his bishop's position by an Englishman in 1891, at the time of his death. In his career, therefore, Crowther illustrates the changing view of the role of Africans in government and church as seen by Europeans.

The experiences of *James Africanus Beale Horton*, also referred to earlier concerning the establishment of the Sierre Leone freed-slave colony, reflects a similar ambivalence about African rights to self-government. Horton, in the generation after that of Crowther's became a medical officer, involved in both Nigeria and the British sphere of the Gold Coast (modern-day Ghana). Horton espoused two principals: first, that there were no physical or intellectual differences between Africans and Europeans; and, second, that the process of social improvement occurring along the West African coast was destined to end in the establishments of free African nations. Serving as a medical officer in the British army, he rose to the rank of lieutenant-colonel before the end of his career in 1880. While in the service, he published a book, *West African Countries and Peoples*, calling for the eventual creation of independent African-run governments in Sierre Leone, the mouth of the Gambia River, and along the Gold Coast. His ideas were carried forward in another book, *Vindication of the African Race*. He was involved in the movement to create a Fanti Confederation on the Gold Coast, a self-governing part of the British sphere of influence. As seen in the case of Bishop Crowther, with the coming of the Scramble for Africa, British opinion turned against African self-government and reverted to the establishment of British colonial domination.

Such early ideas of African nationalism and rights to self-government were furthered by one of the most important precursors of African nationalism, *Edward Wilmot Blyden*. Blyden in his varied career became editor of the first newspaper in Liberia, *The Liberia Herald*, in the 1850s, and became a renowned processor of classics at Liberia College as well. Probably of Hausa background, Blyden taught that each race had its own particular assets to contribute to the well-being of all people. Africans, he believed, should not try to copy or become Europeans. Rather, there was a distinct "African Personality." Blyden based his concept of *Africanness* on three basic principles:

- The concept of Community. Africans placed a special emphasis on the human community and interpersonal relations related to the practice of such community.

- Consonance with nature. Africans lived more in harmony with the natural world than did Europeans, who were more associated with technological dominance over nature.

- Communion with God. Finally, Blyden held that a strong spiritual strength permeates traditional African cultures and values.

Hence, the African contribution to the human community as a whole lay in the three principles of Community, Consonance, and Communion.

The Pan-African Movement

The ideas of Bishop Crowther, Horton, and Blyden, along with other early West Africans, laid the foundation for the development of *Pan-Africanism* after the start of the twentieth century. The Pan-African Movement had its antecedents in the early response to the European occupations of so much of the African continent and their imposition of colonial regimes for exploitation of African resources and people. The first attempt at an international conference on the theme of Pan-Africanism was organized by a London attorney (barrister, technically) names Harry Sylvester Williams, born in Trinidad in the British West Indies. This first conference convened in London in 1900 and was attended by the man who would become the recognized father of the Pan-African Movement, William Edward Burghart (W. E. B.) DuBois. DuBois attended Fisk College (now university) when unable to get funding for Harvard, but eventually was graduated from Harvard and entered graduate school in 1890. He studied at the University of Berlin for two years but was forced to return and complete his degree at

Harvard, again due to funding problems. He became embroiled in a controversy with Booker T. Washington, from Tuskegee Institute, at this time over the question of gradualism in gaining Black rights—the policy favored by Washington but opposed by DuBois. This conflict led to DuBois' book *The Souls of Black Folks*. Out of this controversy came the Niagara Movement and the subsequent founding of the NAACP (the National Association for the Advancement of Colored People), with DuBois as Director of Publications and Research, and the later editor of its publication, *The Crisis*.

At the end of World War I, DuBois revived the idea of a Pan-African Congress, to be held in Paris during the Versaille Peace Conference in an effort to bring before the Versaille delegates the needs of African peoples. The African representative in the French national assembly, Blaise Diagne from the West African French colony of Senegal, was instrumental in persuading the French Government to allow the Pan-African meeting to proceed.

Monument to DuBois at his Final Home, Ghana

Diagne's influence arose from his actions in raising thousands of African troops from French West Africa to fight in the trenches for France during World War I.

Subsequent Pan-African Congresses were held in 1921, 1923, and in 1926–1927. The platform of this early Pan-African Movement seems quite moderate in comparison to later demands for African independence:

- A code of international law applicable for all colonial territories;
- A recognition that African land was held in trust for the future benefit of African people rather than white settlers;
- Regulations on the developments of capitalism in Africa;
- The abolition of slavery, forced labor, and capital punishment in the colonies;
- Increased education for the African people in the colonies;
- Growth in African participation in African colonial governments.

The Fifth Pan-African Congress was held in London at the end of World War II, again under the presidency of DuBois. By that time, the results of the war, with the exhaustion of the main colonial powers of Britain, France, and Belgium and the rise to power of two anti- or at least non-colonial superpowers, gave hope that the end of colonial rule in Africa was in sight. Prominent at this congress were many of the first generation of leaders of the states that did become independent over the following fifteen years. The Pan-African Congresses, therefore, provided inspiration and leadership for the growth of nationalism throughout the continent during the first half of the twentieth century.

The Nationalist Movement in Nigeria

We have noted that the nationalist movements tended to move through stages from initial resistance to protests to the formation of elite-led political organizations. In Nigeria, the first development of nationalist and elite political organization was in the city of Lagos, as the colonial capital and major city. The nationalists in Lagos kept up a campaign against the policies of Lord Lugard, especially the amalgamation of Southern with Northern Nigeria in 1914. Around the time of World War I, the editor of the Lagos Weekly Herald, a man named Thomas H. Jackson, spearheaded this opposition. The early nationalist program in Lagos attacked, on one hand, the racial arrogance of the British colonial officials, and, on the other, called for the institution of British parliamentary-style politics. The nationalists saw the Western educated Africans as the most fit to run a modern state, and yet at the same time, opposed the disrespect shown for traditional African institutions.

In the 1920s the political leadership passed to Herbert Macaulay, who became know as HM. Macaulay organized protests against colonial policies that took a high-handed approach to traditional rulers. When the British colonial administration decided to allow Africans to elect four of the members of the colonial Legislative Council (LegCo, the body that advised the colony's Governor as a sort of quasi-legislative body), Macaulay had an organization ready to respond, becoming the first major political party.

Both Thomas Jackson and Herbert Macaulay were part of a Westernized class who dominated early nationalist politics, many of them descendants of the "re-captives" settled in Sierre Leone at Freetown in the previous century. In Nigeria, they were mostly of Igbo and Yoruba descent, like Crowther and Horton, and looked to Western, especially British models for political and social ideals. As these early cases show, they were ambivalent about traditional rulers and culture. Often, they saw traditionalists as backward and old-fashioned, inadequate to the running of a modern political state. On the other hand, they felt the need to show solidarity with African rulers in their disputes with the colonial bureaucracy. This dilemma reflects one of the political issues engendered by Britain's policy of indirect rule.

Macaulay's party, founded to contest the LegCo seats mentioned above, was completely successful in electing its candidates from 1923 to 1938. Then HM's party was challenged by a more militant brand of nationalism, represented by one of the great leaders of Nigerian nationalist politics, Nnamdi *Azikiwe*. Azikiwe, an Igbo, got his college education at Lincoln College in Pennsylvania. Upon returning to Nigeria in the 1930s, he became a journalist (like Thomas Jackson a generation earlier) and newspaper owner. As editor of the *West African Pilot*, he led the attack against colonial abuses. In 1938, Azikiwe became a force in the newly organized political party, the Nigerian Youth Movement, which challenged Macaulay's organization. In 1941, he took the lead in organizing so-called "tribal unions" into a new, much larger political party: the *National Council of Nigeria and the Cameroons*, the NCNC. This party represents the beginning of truly mass-based, national political organization among the Nigerian nationalists. As a gesture toward solidarity, the now elderly Macaulay was made president of the organization, but the actual running of the party lay in the hand of Azikiwe as the Executive Secretary.

Post-World War II Developments

World War II marked a watershed in the development of African nationalism and movement toward African independence. Both Great Britain and France were significantly weakened by the war despite being on the winning side. The two new superpowers, as we have seen, the United States and the Union of the Soviet Socialist Republics (the USSR) were not colonial powers in Africa nor were they particularly sympathetic to the continuation of colonies there. Within fifteen years of the close of the war, most of the colonies in West Africa had become independent nations.

Nigerians had fought on the British side in the war in the Asian theater of operations (the Burma campaign) as had soldiers from the Gold Coast and Kenya. They expected better treatment from the white governments when they returned from the war, but were often disappointed. Azikiwe's NCNC launched a series of public protests against a new constitution put in place for Nigeria after the war. This new set of rules continued the policy of indirect rule, still giving preference to traditional authorities despite the growing political presence of urban and mass-based organizations such as new labor unions. During these years, the NCNC began to lose some of its radical image as its local branches came under control of teachers, businessmen, and other moderate elements of the newly emerging Nigerian middle class.

Meanwhile larger political parties began to take shape in the other parts of the colony, beyond the stronghold of the NCNC in the predominantly Igbo area of the east. The British reorganized the colony's structure into three large regions: the Northern Region, dominated by the Hausa-Fulani; the Western Region, predominantly Yoruba; and the Eastern Region, encompassing the Igbo heartland.

Traditional ruling elites, based on the Fulani emirates, came to dominate early political organizations in the north. The political head of this movement was a descendant of Uthman dan Fodio, *Ahmadu Bello*, the *Sardauna of Sokoto* (councilor to the Sultan). The administrative management of the new political party of the north was *Abubakar Tafewa Balewa*. He was destined to become the first prime minister of Nigeria when independence did arrive in 1960. Born into a family of small office-holders under the ruler of one of the emirates, he was sent to college to earn a westernized education.

After being graduated from Katsina College, he became the headmaster of an elementary school. Many early nationalists came from the ranks of either journalism or educationists. After completing a degree in London in 1946, he was appointed to the Emir's Council, a body advisory to the administration of the Northern Region. Although he occasionally spoke out against the corruption and inefficiency of the so-called "Native Authorities" (the traditional rulers), he stopped short of calling for their abolition. Balewa played a leading role in forming the major political party of the north, the *Northern People's Congress*, or *NPC*.

The northerners were not entirely monolithic in following the lead of the emirs and their advisers. Another important early nationalist in the north was Aminu Kano, who represented a more liberal trend in politics. He came from a patrician class of Fulani scholars. Like Balewa, he was educated in a local college and then in London. While in Britain, he was favorably impressed by the British Labour Party and tended to support the interests of workers and urban migrants from the countryside. When the Sardauna made the NPC essentially a party for the traditional Hausa-Fulani ruling elites, he forced Aminu Kano out of the party. Kano went on to form his own party, the Northern Elements Political Union, or NEPU. The 1950 manifesto of his party clearly shows that there was opposition to the dominance of the Hausa-Fulani rulers. All parties are but the expression of the class interests, and as the interest of the Talakawa [term for the common people in Hausa] is diametrically opposed to the interests of all sections of the master class [Hausa-Fulani ruling elite], the party seeking the emancipation of the Talakawa must naturally be opposed to the party of the oppressors.[1]

In the southwest, the new Western Region, another new political leader came to the fore in the late 1940s. Obafemi Awolowo had been a chief in the colonial administration, a successful cocoa grower, and businessman. In 1950, while the NPC was growing in the north, Awolowo formed the Action Group (the AG), relying on the support of Yoruba professionals, businessmen, and some *Obas*.

The new political organization grew out of a Yoruba cultural organization, which had been created just in 1948. As a result, the non-Yoruba elements in the Western Region began to look to the NCNC for support, fearing domination by the AG, identified with the Yoruba. In the area nearer to the Niger River, around the old city of Benin and the Delta, some called for the creation of a new Midwestern Region, to avoid domination by the Yoruba as well.

The Growth of Regionalism

Regionalism and its conflicts were inherited from the colonial period. As early as the amalgamation of the northern region with the southern, the main lines of fissure emerged. The southerners, both in the west and in the east, tended to look on the north as backward and potentially threatening. The northerners in their turn feared the domination of the more educated and westernized southerners. Unfortunately, through a series of colonial constitutions leading up to independence, the British perpetuated the notion of federalism and, therefore, separate regional autonomy.

These series of colonial constitutions go back to 1922, which set up the first elections for African representatives to LegCo, as we saw with the formation of Macaulay's political party. The first constitution after World War II brought all of Nigeria, including the north, under a colony-wide LegCo for the first time. A new constitution, formally recognizing the domination of each region by the large ethnic groups, came into place in 1951. Regional governments and assemblies were put into place for the first time. When a British government official expressed his concern that this new arrangement would promote regional loyalties in Nigeria, the governor responsible for putting in place the new constitution wrote as follows:

> I feel, however, that any such tendency would be quickly corrected by the nature of a Minister's work at the centre. He will have to deal with questions of a Nigeria-wide nature, and, also, on occasion, with questions in which his region might not be directly concerned. The effect of this would be to instill into him a Nigerian habit of thought. . .[2]

The reality that brought home the weakness of the Governor's reasoning was the political uproar that greeted a national assembly member's introduction of a motion calling for independence by 1956. Before allowing consideration of independence, the northern representatives demanded even more restrictions on the power of the central government to prevent any tampering with the privileges of Hausa-Fulani elite. But, a new constitution introduced in 1954 provided even more regional autonomy than its predecessors. For example, judiciaries became regionally based. The institutiom of "customary" courts, including Islamic or *shari'a* courts, was left to each region. The central government would be responsible only for defense, foreign affairs, and collecting customs duties. We shall see later how the institution of *shari'a* law in the northern states has led to continuing conflicts in Nigeria.

In 1957, the year in which Ghana became the first sub-Saharan African state to gain independence, Nigerians elected their first colony wide, African prime minister. In that year also, a motion passed the federal House calling for independence for Nigeria in 1959. Great Britain agreed to October of 1960. The elections that would determine the government that would lead the newly independent state were scheduled for 1959.

The Arrival of Independence

Clearly, the lines of disunity were in place as the nationalists began to debate the basis for Nigeria's transition to independence from Great Britain. These lines of opposition were reinforced by regional, ideological, ethnic, and religious divisions. The north was dominated by a traditional elite, whose power had its origins in the policies of Lord Lugard as well as the Sultanate of Sokoto and the jihads of Uthman dan Fodio. The Western Region was dominated by the AG of Chief Awolowo, representing in a large measure the interests of the newly prosperous westernized elites of that region. In the Eastern Region, the mass-based political party of Azikiwe, the NCNC, was dominant. There were oppositions groups in each region, as smaller groups feared domination by the larger. The independence process was delayed during the 1950s by the competitions among these points of view. The NCNC tended to favor a more centralized form of government, while the other parties held out for a looser, federal type of structure, leaving some autonomy to each region.

By 1959, most elements including the British colonial government had agreed to a constitution based on regional federalism. As one would expect, the constitution was modeled on the British parliamentary system, with the head of government being the leader of the party holding a majority in the national assembly. In the elections, the NPC, representing the largest part of the country, won the most seats but fell well short of a majority. Given the parliamentary model, the only way to organize a government required two or more parties' forming a coalition to reach a majority. The NPC (of the north) and the NCNC (Azikiwe's party of the east) joined in such a coalition and formed the first government of Nigeria, with Balewa as Prime Minister and Azikiwe as Governor-General (ceremonial head of state).

Summary

The roughly sixty years that Nigeria was a colony of Great Britain had profound effects, central to the contemporary problems facing the country today. In many ways, Nigeria shared these colonial effects with other African states gobbled up by the imperial scramble. The persistent effects of the colonial experience can be seen in the continuation of a dependent economy and difficulties of national integration, militating against a solid national identity.

The colonial economy was originally based on the production and export of a few raw materials. This type of economy, based on primary commodities, relied on largely unskilled labor. Manufacturing and processing industries remain undeveloped or even completely absent. Capital for the development of cash crop farming and mining came mainly from overseas, usually from the metropolitan power; consequently, more of the profits flowed overseas, as well. Public expenditures by the colonial government, as we have seen, went primarily for development of roads, railroads, harbors, and other infrastructure to facilitate the extraction of the raw materials. The funding of education was therefore left largely to philanthropic institutions, such as religious missions.

Throughout most of Africa, this economic system resulted in societies with small, literate elites in urban areas and masses of unskilled laborers, who spent part of their time in urban areas and part in rural villages.

By 1960, the year of Nigerian independence, two-thirds of Africa's exports were agricultural commodities, with cocoa, groundnuts, palm products, coffee and cotton, the most important. Whole regions became dependent on the world markets for a single commodity. When the prices for cocoa or palm oil fell, devastating results ensured for local economies. Furthermore, when an area depended upon a single crop for major earnings, the threats of crop disease, poor weather, insects, and so one were magnified. When food production suffered, newly urbanized populations who could not grow their own food suffered disproportionately. Cassava, for that reason, as a cheap if not particularly nutritious food, has become central to the Nigerian diet.

National integration was made more difficult by colonial policies. Colonies were not created on the basis of traditional ethnic or geographic boundaries. Within a large colony such as Nigeria, hundreds of ethnic groups were put together to be ruled as a single colony rather than nation. Indirect rule, as implemented by the British authorities, favored some groups over others. In areas dominated by large ethnic groups—the Hausa-Fulani in the north, the Igbo in the east, and Yoruba in the west—serious conflicts were inevitable. Nigeria at independence faced the formidable task of creating a feeling of national unity where neither nation nor unity had existed before.

References

1. Cited in Basil Davidson, *The Black Man's Burden: Africa and the Curse of the Nation-State*. New York: Times Books, 1992, p. 109.

2. Correpondence between Sir John Macpherson (Governor) and James Griffiths, Secretary of State for the Colonies, 15 April 1951, Doc. J45 A132, Africana Collection, Boston University.

CHAPTER SEVEN

Independence and Aftermath

On October 1, 1960, Nigeria became the fourth most populous member of the British Commonwealth, behind India, Pakistan, and the United Kingdom itself. Creating national unity in the newly independent state faced even more serious obstacles in the early 1960s. Because each of the three regions had its own government, parliament, prime minister, and so forth, confusion arose over who was responsible for national affairs. Relationships among the various regional leaders were complicated. Often the more optimistic expectations for independence were frustrated. The gap between the wealthy elite and the mass of the population grew wider with each year, and politicians seemed more interested in enriching themselves and their families than in developing the nation. Younger politicians and professionals seemed disappointed with the conservative line taken by Prime Minister Balewa in international affairs. These frustrations coupled with regionalism and ethnic divisiveness built toward a crisis.

In the over 45 years since independence, Nigeria has experienced a bewildering number of different governments, political parties, and heads of government. Although the long list of names and political parties may seem hopelessly daunting, the overall picture has remained fairly clear. The regional, ethnic, and religious lines of division, reinforced during the colonial period, have dominated politics since independence. A second equally clear generalization is that military coups and military governments have recurred with disturbing frequency. Each attempt at restoring civilian and democratic government has seemed to fail, although at the time of the writing of this edition, an elected civilian president was in office, although in fact this president comes from the ranks of the military, had himself participated in earlier military coups, and had been at one time head of the state under a military regime.

Divisions in the Newly Independent State

As we saw at the end of the previous chapter, Nigeria entered upon independence with no political party holding a majority in the national parliament. The northern party, the Northern Peoples' Congress, or NPC, was in a dominant position, having won more seats in the house than any other. The two largest parties, in terms of members elected, together comprised a majority and so formed a coalition government. This coalition consisted of the NPC and the political party of Nnamdi Azikiwe, the National Council of Nigerian Citizens (the new name for the Igbo-dominated party known as the NCNC). Azikiwe assumed the largely ceremonial title of Governor-General (meaning representative of the Queen of Great Britain, who, as in Canada or Australia, was recognized the Head of the State). The political or real power of the government was wielded by the Prime Minister, Sir Abubakar Alhaji Tafewa Balewa. The Yoruba-dominated party of the Western Region, the Action Group, or AG, under Chief Obafemi Awolowo, became the official party of opposition. There could have been several pragmatic reasons behind Azikiwe's decision to align with Hausa-Fulani north and not the Yoruba of the west. First, he probably believed that his party, the NCNC, could compete successfully for votes in the west but not in the north. If he had aligned with the AG in the west, the nature of coalition politics would have ruled out such competition there for votes. There was also the danger than an east-west coalition against the north would have hardened the north-south split. In that case, Azikiwe feared exacerbating such divisiveness could endanger the many Igbo living in the Northern Region. These considerations reveal the nature of regionalist politics in the new nation. Shifting lines of competition among the three regions became the dominant theme of what Nigerians now call the First Republic.

The population of the Northern Region gave it dominance in national politics—this was the major fault-line of Nigeria politics. In 1962 a new census triggered a major crisis. The previous census, completed under the British government back in the 1950s, indicated the Northern Region had a slightly larger population than the two southern regions combined. Southerners always questioned this result, given their fear of domination by the conservative, Hausa-Fulani north. When the new census appeared to give even more of an advantage to the Northern Region, a controversy erupted that led to the dissolution of the coalition of the northern NPC and the southeastern NCNC.

Meanwhile, further trouble developed in the Western Region. Awolowo intended to make the Action Group, the AG, a truly national party, contesting seats in all regions of the country. On the other hand, Awolowo's chief deputy, a man named Samuel Akintola, wanted to concentrate on holding onto power in the west, while cooperating with the national coalition at the federal level. The rivalry between these two leaders reflected the sort of power struggles taking place in other regions as well. It would be a mistake to think of each region as wholly monolithic, even within the dominant ethnic group.

Some of the major traditional Yoruba rulers and wealthy businessmen backed the more regionalist and conservative agenda of Akintola. His support came mainly from the northern areas of Yorubaland. Awolowo's support, on the other hand, came from southern areas, closer to the larger cities, especially Lagos, the areas considered to be more "modernized." The NPC, the northern party, saw its interests on the side of supporting the traditional elements against the more popular Awolowo.

The ruling coalition of the NPC and NCNC sought to weaken the position of Awolowo further by creating a new, fourth state, the Midwestern Region around Benin City and extending to the Niger River. This new state was carved out of an area that seemed to support Chief Awolowo. When Awolowo backed public demonstrations in the west against actions of the federal government which seemed to favor his rivals, he and thirty of his closest supporters were charged with treason and imprisoned. Awolowo himself, late in 1962, was sentenced to 10 years in prison as a result of these charges. The situation in the Western Region began to approach civil war.

On October 1, 1963, three years after independence, the federal government dominated by the NPC successfully enacted a new constitution replacing the Queen with a Federal President (again, largely a ceremonial position in a parliamentary systems). The new post went to the grand old man of Nigerian politics, Nnamdi Azikiwe. More importantly, the new constitution meant there had to be new elections, which were set for 1964. New political parties would be formed to contest the new elections. But, essentially, these new parties were simply incarnations of the former, regionally based ones. There were some realignments growing out of the disputes we have been reviewing. For example, Awolowo's opponents in the Western Region joined with northern party, the old NPC. Awolowo's followers, on the other hand, joined with the southern-oriented party that grew out the old NCNC. This latter party, protesting the legitimacy of how the elections were to be held, tried to boycott the new elections. The northern party again dominated the new parliament and central government as a result.

The following year, there were regional government elections—or at least attempts to hold regional government elections. In the west, the supporters of Awolowo believed that the northern leaders tried to manipulate the results (given their control of the national, central government), violence broke out. Eventually, two different outcomes were reported, leading to a further breakdown of law and order in the Western Region.

The First Coups and the Biafran Civil War

Would the centrifugal forces of regionalism, ethnic rivalry, and religious differences tear the new nation apart? Increasingly, that was the question given the disputes of the first few years. Under circumstances of disorder and confusion, a group of army majors, mostly Igbo and led by an Igbo officer, staged a military coup on the night of January 14–15, 1966. Soldiers killed several prominent national leaders, including the Prime Minister, Tafewa Balewa, the Sardauna of Soloto, Prime Minister of the Northern Region and leader of the Hausa-Fulani, and Samuel Akintola, the rival of Awolowo and Prime Minister of the Western Region. No leading Igbo leaders were killed. The majors were themselves unable to establish a government, so the remaining top army generals took over under the leadership of General I. T. U. Ironsi, also an Igbo. The National Military Government suspended the constitution and placed military governors in charge of each of the four regions.

In May, General Ironsi abolished the regions in order to replace the federal system with a unitary, centralized state. All political parties were outlawed and the formation of new parties prohibited for the time being.

When Ironsi failed to punish the mostly Igbo coup leaders for the murders that took place during the coup, and when he promulgated a centralized government seen as favoring southerners over northerners, the Northern Region erupted in anger. Attacks against Igbos in the north killed thousands, and thousands more began streaming back toward the Igbo heartland in the southeast. Then in July General Ironsi himself was killed on a visit to Ibadan in a northern-led counter-coup. On August 1, 1966, Yakubu Gowon, a lieutenant-colonel from one of the small ethnic groups in the Middle Belt (the region between the Niger and Benue Rivers and the north) became the new head of the government. The military governor of the Eastern Region, another lieutenant-colonel, named Odemegwu Ojukwu, refused to recognize Gowon as either head of the military or of the government. Meanwhile, during September and October as many as 30,000 Igbo were killed in the Northern Region, while as many as two million people fled as refugees to the Eastern Region. If these events had occurred later in the century, no doubt they would have been described as "ethnic cleansing."

Clearly, there was going to be a show-down between Gowon, wanting a strong federal state under his control, and Ojukwu, wanting a looser confederation. In May of 1967, Gowon attempted to break up the regional groupings that had proved so troublesome by creating 12 new states, cutting across old boundaries in an attempt to break up the power of the former regions. Ojukwu rejected this plan and immediately declared the Eastern Region the new, independent Republic of Biafra (in fact, the Eastern Region had been acting as an independent region since March). While most of the Igbo of the Eastern Region appeared to support secession, many of the coastal peoples did not. As a further complication, oil from the delta and coastal region was becoming the most important export for Nigeria. The petroleum industry was located in the area claimed by the new state of Biafra.

Civil War: Biafra

Civil war was not long in coming, as Gowon'g government intended to bring the oil-rich Biafra back into the federation. Actual hostilities broke out in July of 1967, marked by initial successes by Biafran troops in repulsing the federal army's invasion. A column of the Biafran army, led by an officer named Victor Banjo, who was himself a Yoruba, crossed the Niger River into the Midwestern State and occupied the city of Benin. Both the federal and Biafran sides feared that Banjo would declare an independent state there as well, or at least, strike out on his own in an effort to take over Nigeria (Ojukwu may also have had such national ambitions).

The military commander of the Western Region, now threatened by Banjo's army, was a man who will reappear throughout the rest of this text, Olusegun Obasanjo, later President of the Republic of Nigeria. Banjo sent messages to Obasanjo, notably through the Nobel-prize winning playwright, Wole Soyinka, hoping Obasanjo would allow Banjo's army through to the capital city of Lagos to take over the Nigerian government. Obasanjo sided with the central government, leading to Banjo's eventual defeat and execution and to Soyinka's imprisonment for the rest of the civil war.[1]

Instead of ending quickly in 1967, the civil war dragged on for three very long, very bloody years. The federal government blockaded the east in an effort to force Biafra to end its seccession (reminiscent of the U.S. Government's blockade of the Confederate States during the American Civil War). The Ojukwu government hired the international public relations firm of Markpress of Geneva to portray the blockade as an attempt to starve the

Biafran civilians into submission. In fact, world public opinion became a major factor on both sides in the struggle. Gowon's government, aware of the negative image of starving children in Biafra, tried to send food and medical relief in through land corridors, but the Biafran Government would allow only airlifted supplies from their own sources.

The Biafran War became an international issue, as various nations took sides. Great Britain supported and provided military assistance to the federal side, as did the Soviet Union. France and South Africa (then under control of a white-minority government) tended to give rhetorical support to Biafra and, in some cases, through smuggled arms shipments, tangible support. South Africa was probably motivated by a desire to weaken the potentially strongest Black African nation, which could become a dangerous opponent to that government's *apartheid* regime. Richard Nixon, who became President of the United States in 1969, during the civil war, seemed to favor recognition of Biafra and mediation to end the conflict. One the other hand, Henry Kissinger, Nixon's influential Secretary of State, did not want the conflict to distract America's attention from what he considered more important matters, such as settling the conflict in Viet Nam. The State Department always appeared to favor the federal side. As a result of these differing views, the U.S. took a basically neutral position. Among African states, only four recognized Biafra: Tanzania and Zambia (English-speaking former British colonies), and Gabon and Ivory Coast (French-speaking former French colonies).

Gradually, the federal army, under the command of Obasanjo, encircled the last remaining pockets of Biafran resistance in the Igbo heartland. Gowon made a major effort to prevent mistreatment or any appearance of retaliation that could be construed as genocide against the Igbo people. Azikiwe, who had remained out of the country during the war, returned to Lagos and proclaimed his belief that the Nigerian army would not slaughter the Biafrans after the war.

Following thirty months of civil war, in January of 1970, Ojukwu fled the country, leaving his second-in-command to announce that Biafra no longer existed. Former rebel officers and civil servants were allowed to resume their posts and food relief flowed into the Igbo enclave. The government quickly distributed seed and farm tools to rebuild the agricultural base. Gowon and the victorious Nigerian Army were magnanimous and conciliatory toward former enemies, and fears of retaliation were allayed. The

Nigerian-Biafran Civil War, however, is still remembered as one of the major tragedies of newly-independent Africa.

Summary of First Coups and Biafra

The ordeals of Nigeria in its first decade of independence (the 1960s) are representative of many of the problems facing most new African nations in that time. The obstacles behind these troubles include the following:

1. An economic infrastructure intended to serve colonial rather than national interests. Road and railway systems, for example, were built to facilitate the extraction of raw materials from the colony, rather than to link Nigeria to a wider West African market. The routes, therefore, all run north and south rather than east and west.

2. Restrictions on national political development during the colonial period. Colonial rule did not seek to develop political leaders who could take over the administration of the entire nation. Administration was geared toward serving the interests of the colonial government.

3. Over-emphasis on ethnic and regional politics in colonial and early-independent phases of national life. This emphasis derived from a "divide-and-conquer" strategy used by the colonial power. The British policy of "indirect rule" perpetuated traditional divisions and ethnic units.

Overall, colonization was intended to benefit the ruling nation in Europe, in this case, Great Britain, and to provide it with cheap raw materials and a market for Britain's own manufactured goods. As a result, the new nations throughout the continent were often unprepared to establish the institutional and economic bases for nationhood.

The Second Decade: The Coups Continue

In Nigeria, as well as much of the rest of Africa, frustrations with the political process led to a series of military coups and military governments. After the military victory over Biafra in 1970, Gowon announced a return to civilian rule scheduled for 1975. Just before that date, however, Gowon himself was overthrown in another military coup. Coups have continued since, followed by attempts to return to democratic, civilian government, followed by more coups.

During the 1970s, Nigeria began to play a more influential role in Africa and international affairs in general. Oil production expanded and after the civil war, in 1971, Nigeria joined the international Organization of Petroleum Exporting Countries, or OPEC. Nigeria became the seventh largest oil producing nation (now eleventh). Petroleum exports increased even more with the Arab-led oil embargo against western nations following the so-called "Yom Kippur" war between Israel and Arab states in 1973.

Unfortunately, increased government corruption and diversion of public funds for private use also marked the first half of the 1970s. The state governors (increased to 12 in number) were particularly notorious for alleged misuse of power and public funds. The professional army commanders, who had helped win the civil war and who had been instrumental in Gowon's rise to power, began to lose respect for the military president during this time. The leader of these commanders was Murtala Mohammed, representing a group of younger, professionally trained administrators known informally as the "Kaduna Mafia." (Kaduna is the home of the Nigerian Defense Academy for officer-training.) Although largely drawn from the conservative north with links to the aristocratic Hausa-Fulani, this group generally sees itself as nationalist and reformist. It was Murtala Mohammed who led the coup against Gowon in 1975 and became the military head of government, vested in a Supreme Military Council.

The new military government under Murtala Mohammed faced the same kind of divisive issues that had earlier torn the country apart together with controversies surrounding a new population census, the question of when to return to civilian rule, and creation of a new federal capital in the center of the country at Abuja. Although Mohammed was the leader, the military council operated on a collegial basis, which meant that when Mohammed was assassinated in an abortive coup in 1976, a new supreme commander, this time General Obasanjo, could pick up and continue most of the same policies. This is, of course, the same Obasanjo who had commanded the army in the civil war, and who was later to be elected president again. Obasanjo's government continued its campaign against corrupt officials: ten of the former twelve state governors were found guilty of massive corruption and, in "Operation Deadwoods," about 10,000 public employees were dismissed from office. The Mohammed-Obasanjo administration is remembered as probably the most benign of the military governments of Nigeria. The international airport in Lagos today is named in honor of Murtala Mohammed.

At this point, then, there have been three military coups (plus one attempted coup resulting in the death of Murtala Mohammed). At this point, then, we should explain how a military regime usually works. Under a military government the constitution is suspended if not abolished outright. Nigeria's first military government, under Gowon, took over legislative, executive, and even judicial functions for a time. In 1970, by decree of the military government, the judiciary became independent and remained so under Mohammed-Obasanjo regime as well. Under military government, laws are enacted by decree of the supreme commander instead of by a legislature and executive. The military appoints a military commander to be governor of each region. Of course, the military could not govern alone: the civil service was required to handle the day-to-day affairs and operations. Consequently, the military formed a sort of partnership with the civil servants and some business and professional leaders. A national-level executive council discussed or recommended some policy and included some civilian representation (more like a colonial LegCo; see Chapter Five).

To enhance its control of the country, the Mohammed-Obsanjo regime expanded the number of states from the 12 under Gowon to 19 (later expanded to 30 in 1994). They hoped that a larger number of states would dilute regional hegemony of the major ethnic groups, which had bedeviled Nigerian politics since independence. In addition, smaller states would be less self-sufficient and therefore more dependent on the central government. Through its control of oil revenues, which by 1976 had become 93 percent of Nigeria's total export income, the central government accumulated a great deal of income which it could distribute as largess. Increasing the number of states also increased the bureaucracy with 19 state administrations in place of the original three at the time of independence.

The Return to Civilian Government: The Second Republic

When the military takes power in Africa, they generally see their rule as temporary, a corrective to remedy the ills of an unpopular or corrupt civilian regime. In a sense, the temporary nature of military governments allows for a form of permanence. Since it is conceivable that civilian regimes will always need "correction," the military can always return to power. This pattern has repeated itself not only in Nigeria, but in Ghana, Uganda, and many other African nations.

When Murtala Mohammed came to power, he immediately announced plans for a return to civilian government. After Mohammed's death, Obasanjo held to the initial time table for turning government back to an elected administration in 1979. The military insisted, however, on laying down rules for political participation in the new republic. After all, the military did not really want a civilian government too different ideologically from its own regime. Some argue that his "ideology" is virtually an absence of ideology, because control of government is mainly seen as a way to gain access to wealth. Nonetheless, an important feature of the military's rules for the transfer of power was control over the creation of new political parties. A federal commission would determine which parties would be allowed to participate in the process.

A constituent assembly began work on a new constitution in December of 1976. This body was a collection of "wise men," including former politicians, businessmen, lawyers, university professors, and other members of the political and economic elite. For the most part, peasants, farmers, labor union members, students, and women were excluded from the process. The new constitution, completed in 1978, added to the power of the central government, in comparison with the earlier constitutions, following the tendency of military governments. The assembly set in place a system of checks and balances among the legislative, executive, and judicial branches, as in the American constitution. In addition to the civil rights of citizens, such as freedom of speech and religion, there were to be socioeconomic rights, which included rights to education, economic development, and a just economic order. These socioeconomic rights, however, were considered to be long-range goals, not yet actually enforceable by courts. That is, while a citizen could go to court to seek redress for a violation of his or her civil rights, the citizen could not do so when economic rights had been violated.

This new constitution, after some modifications by the military, became the basis for the elections of 1979 for the return to civilian government. To an outsider, the details of the ensuing campaign and election appear very complicated, so the following discussion is offered as a short summary to illustrate the nature of Nigerian politics during this period.

Two rules were put in place for electing a new president. First, the new president needed to do more than simply get more votes than his opponents (all the candidates were male). To demonstrate a national following, the successful candidate had to receive at least one-fourth of the votes cast in two-thirds of the 19 states. The intent was to avoid a purely regional candidate. Second, only political parties vetted and approved by the Federal Election Commission could field candidates. This second rule meant only registered parties could participate, freezing out independent candidates or those from special interest groups, such as labor unions.

Despite the new regulations, the major parties formed for these elections closely resembled the earlier regional parties from the north, southwest, and southeast. For example, the largest party, although called the National Party of Nigeria, the NPN, had its primary support in the north. Chief Awolowo formed a party also intended to be national, but based largely on support from the west, especially from the Yoruba. Azikiwe, despite his age, formed a similar part based on eastern support.

In the event, the candidate from the north, Shehu Shagari, won the election with the requisite distribution of votes in the 19 states. Awolowo was a close second in terms of total votes, but 4.3 million of his total of 4.9 million votes came from four Yoruba-dominated states. Local and state elections continued to reflect ethnic and regional politics.

Economic conditions deteriorated during Shagari's administration. A world oil glut, in contrast to the days of OPEC's oil embargo, drove down petroleum revenues while growing corruption and inefficiency siphoned away state funds from education, development, and other services. Shagari's political party derived its power from its ability to deliver "chop" (payoffs, bribes, and the like) to notables and party stalwarts. The decline in national revenues also weakened the political power base of the power, as a result. As one observer of this period of Nigerian politics puts it, "Even while politicians continued to consume flagrantly, raise their personal emoluments and live in an unprecedently lavish style . . ., the population were subject to worker 'retrenchments,' higher taxes, declining services, and inflation."[2]

Under these rather unpromising conditions, the 1983 elections went forward. The ruling party, now in control of the governmental apparatus, could use its muscle to weaken opponents by excluding some and buying off others. Candidates started shifting from party to party to find a slot in a winning combination. This shifting around was possible because the parties were really not ideologically based. As a result, although roughly the same candidates and parties contested the elections, party lines and platforms were so unclear, it is hard to analyze the results. In the event, Shagari again won defeating Awolowo and Azikiwe (now both in their 70s), amid charges of voter fraud, rigging the ballots, and so on.

Military Government Re-Installed

The newly elected government lasted only until the end of the election year, 1983. On the last day of that year, the military, now under General Mohammed Buhari, announced they were taking over again. Buhari intended to reassert discipline in political life, in line with the policies of his predecessor, Murtala Mohammed. So-called lazy or incompetent civil servants were fired, and, in some cases, caned; corrupt politicians were investigated and charged. The military based their claim to power, again, on their claimed ability to clean up the mess, while not making fundamental changes in the economic structure of the country. Several coups were in the planning stages in late 1983, and it appears Buhari's may have been launched when it was to forestall those of more junior and radical officers. There were rumors of a second failed coup against Burhari within 100 days of his take-over.

While on the surface, the Buhari coup intended to correct the economic problems of the Shagari administration, in reality Buhari continued many of the policies of his predecessor. He accepted the annual budget as already drawn up by Shagari, for example. He acted to comply with repayment and economic austerity packages imposed by the International Monetary Fund (the IMF), as conditionalities (as they were called) of receiving loans from the international bank. He did find some of the stricter conditions of the World Bank unacceptable, however, and therefore turned down a $3 billion load to cover Nigeria's balance of payments deficit. The result was more austerity for the citizens of Nigeria with no signs of improving economic development. The government became increasingly repressive, instituting the death penalty, by firing squad, for a wide range of offenses.

As this repression grew, many factions in the military became disillusioned with Buhari. Perhaps to forestall other coups again, the army's chief-of-staff, Ibrahim Babangida, overthrew Buhari in yet another military coup in August of 1985. Babangida revealed himself to more conciliatory and effective as a leader than Buhari, and appears to have had more support within the military itself. Of course, his government was still a military dictatorship. Interestingly, while this text was being revised, Babangida appeared to be planning to run for president under the current civilian constitution.

After his coming to power, Babangida began to put in place plans to return the country to an elected civilian government in 1992. He seemed to follow the procedures used by Obasanjo a decade earlier. He set up a new body to draft a constitution and instituted a Center for Democratic Studies for the purpose of training new politicians. In order to avoid some of the earlier problems with Nigerian election (the reason given by Babangida), he banned from politics "old breed" politicians, that is, anyone who participated in the First or Second Republic. And, control over the electoral process was even tighter than in 1979. A federal election commission was to approve two—and only two—political parties for contesting the elections (no other parties were to be allowed). When none that came forward met the criteria set by the military. Babangida decided to create two new "grassroots" parties by decree. Apparently he saw no irony in a grassroots being decreed by the government. Of the two parties thus created, one was required to be slightly to the left of center and one slightly to the right. Perhaps influenced by American politics, the slightly left party was called the Social *Democratic* Party, and the slightly to the right party was called the National *Republican* Convention. The NRC drew most of its support from the north, while the SDP drew its support from the south.

After several false starts, two presidential candidates were selected by these manufactured parties, both of whom had close business and personal ties with President Babangida. Elections were finally held in June of 1993 and seemed to go smoothly according to international observers. Although preliminary reports indicated that the Social Democratic candidate, Moshood Abiola, a wealthy media owner and a Muslim Yoruba, had won handily, Babangida suddenly stepped in and nullified the election results. In the ensuring uproar, the general stepped down, handing over temporary power to a handpicked civilian president, Ernest Shonekan in August of 1993. In that fall, however, General Sani Abacha, long associated with other military coups and governments, staged yet another coup, and returned Nigerian to military rule.

Abacha's regime was even more oppressive than earlier military governments. He fomented international protest and local crisis when his government executed the well-known poet and television producer, Ken Saro-Wiwa, and eight of his colleagues active in a movement protesting violations of human rights and the environment of the Ogoni people. Although they were a very small ethnic group, the Ogoni live in the region of the Niger Delta dominated by the oil industry, represented by such giant firms as Royal-Dutch Shell. The Nobel-laureate Wole Soyinka, imprisoned during the Biafran war, was forced into self-imposed exile during this time as well.

The repression became even harsher when the apparent winner of the 1993 elections, Moshood Abiola, returned to Nigeria to contest his claims to the presidency. He was thrown into prison under harsh conditions despite his poor health and the later murder of his wife, who was killed while campaigning for his cause. The widely-respected former military president, Olusegun Obasanjo, who in the meantime had been an unsuccessful candidate for Secretary General of the United Nations, was also charged with treason, nearly executed, and then placed in prison. Many other respected Nigerian leaders found themselves in jail under Abacha as well. Abacha promised a return to civilian government but with many restrictions and qualifications, while international protests grew louder and louder.

In the summer of 1998, the sudden, unexpected death of Abacha, followed a month later by the equally unexpected death of Moshood Abiola while still in prison, completely altered prospects for the political future. By the October, in 1998, conditions had so improved, following the release of most of the major dissidents from prison, Wole Soyinka returned to Nigeria to a hero's welcome.

As 1998 drew to a close Nigerians hoped for an early end to military rule and return to democratic politics in Nigeria. The following table indicates the dominance of the military and the Hausa-Fulani elite in national politics since independence.

Return to Democratic Government

Following the death of Abacha, the presidency passed to another general, Abdulsalam Abubakar, who was seen by everyone as a caretaker holding the place of president until a new one could be elected. In the elections of 1999, in an unusual turn of events, two Yoruba men were the candidates for national president. The most prominent was Olusegun Obasanjo, who has figured prominently in our narrative since independence. His opponent was Olu Falae, a former prominent banker and graduate of Yale University, who had been national minister of finance under Babangida. Also unusual in this election was the fact that both candidates were Christians. Obasanjo had announced when he was finally released from prison in 1998, that he had become, in fact, a "born again" Christian. Given his former prominence and association with the military, Obasanjo was very successful in winning votes in the Hausa-Fulani north as well as in the southeast (ironically, the former Biafra, which he had conquered as military commander in the civil war). Falae was the overwhelming favorite of voters in the Yoruba west, even though Obasanjo is also a Yoruba.

Obasanjo was re-elected in 2003, this time defeating Muhammed Buhari, the former military dictator of the 1980s who had been overthrown by Babangida. Another candidate against Obasanjo this time was the former president of Biafra, Odumegwu Ojukwu, who had been permitted to return to Nigeria and to participate in politics. This time, Obasanjo swept the southern areas of the country, even among the Yoruba, who had not supported him four years earlier. Some were suspicious of his numbers in some areas of the oil-rich delta, in which he received as much as 100 percent of the reported vote in some constituencies. The north lined up behind Buhari, emphasizing again the regional divide in Nigerian politics. Recall that in 1999, without a Hausa-Fulani in the race, the north had supported Obasanjo, perhaps because of his association with the military, typically controlled by the Hausa-Fulani.

Table 3. Heads of Government, Independent Nigeria

Name	Years	Military/civilian
Abubakar Tafewa Balewa	1960–1966	Civilian
I. T. U. Aguiyi-Ironsi	1966	Military
Yakabu Gowon	1966–1975	Military
Murtala Mohammed	1975–1976	Military
Olusegun Obasanjo	1976–1979	Military
Alhaji Shehu Shagari	1979–1983	Civilian
Muhammed Buhari	1983–1985	Military
Ibrahim Babangida	1985–1993	Military
Ernest Shonekan	1993	Civilian, appointed by Military
Sani Abacha	1993–1998	Military
Adbusalam Abubakar	1998–1999	Military
Olusegun Obsanjo	1999–	Civilian (former military)

These recent events point to two overriding concerns facing Nigeria now and in the future: the impact of oil on Nigeria's political as well as environmental landscape, and the dangerous role of increasing regional, ethnic, and religious tensions. We turn to these two major issues.

Oil and Nigeria

Many Americans are unaware that Nigeria is one of the major overseas suppliers of petroleum to the United States. Some of the sudden increase in the price of gasoline in the U.S. in 2006 was attributed to unrest in the Niger Delta region, due to the fear that it could restrict the flow of oil. Nigeria itself is immensely dependent on the revenues from the sale of oil, which accounts for up to 98 percent of the export earnings of the country. In 2006 money from oil revenues accounted for 83 percent of the government income and expenditures. Oil has become such a major factor in the modern history of Nigeria that it would be impossible to understand events there without some basic understanding of the role the petroleum industry has come to play.

Harvesting Palm Kernels

There is an irony in the current importance of oil in this region, since you may recall that the Niger Delta was called by Europeans in the nineteenth century the "Oil Rivers." The reason for the name then, of course, was unrelated to petroleum oil, but rather referred to palm oil, then a major trade item replacing the trade in slaves that had so dominated the economy of the delta for centuries. Palm oil, a heavy vegetable oil from the fleshy pulp around the palm kernel, had long been used in West Africa for food preparation. The Igbo, in speaking of their fondness for the use of proverbs in their speech, say, "Proverbs are the palm oil with which words are eaten." Industrializing Europe in the 1800s created a demand for African palm oil for two major uses: as a lubricant for machinery and as an ingredient in soap manufacture. Two kinds of oil come from the oil palm tree: the thick oil from the fleshy part of the fruit and the clearer oil found inside the palm kernel itself (which is called "palm kernel oil"). Both palm oil and palm kernel oil became major agricultural products along the West African coast.

The history of trade in palm oil shows similarities with the contemporary experiences with exploitation of petroleum in Nigeria. The trade in both kinds of oil is based on extraction and export of a primary commodity—in one case agricultural and in the other mineral. The control of both trades lay largely in European or non-African hands. In the nineteenth century, the English businessman, Sir George Goldie Taubman (usually known as Goldie) was able to organize the British traders operating in the delta into a single monopoly by 1879, known as the United African Company, afterwards, the Royal Niger Company. Goldie was able to take advantage of the British Government's interest in extending its sphere of influence over the area in rivalry with potential German and French competitors at the time of the beginning of the Scramble for Africa. A royal charter was granted by Her Majesty's Government in 1886 allowing Goldie's representatives to negotiate a series of unequal treaties with local delta chiefs and rulers, mainly of Ijaw, Itsekiri, and Urhobo peoples. Because of the royal charter, Goldie's company, on the model of the British East India Company, was allowed to employ gunboats as well as military and police powers to dominate and control trade in the delta and on the Niger River itself. Local African resentment of the company's high handed dealing with the African palm traders led to some armed rebellions, especially at the African port of Brasstown at the southern point of the delta. The delta peoples' experience with the palm oil trade was a precursor to their resentment and resistance to modern petroleum companies and their activities in late twentieth and early twenty-first centuries.

The African peoples of the delta have thus experienced in the last two centuries a transition from international trade in slaves to, first, palm oil and then to petroleum oil.

Petroleum oil was first discovered in the Niger Delta in 1956 by the Shell-BP Corporation, and the first oil field went into production in 1958. A second oil field came on line near the city of Warri in 1965. The war over the attempted secession by Biafra interrupted these developments, but as soon as the war was over, oil production resumed. In 1971, one year after the end of the war, Nigeria joined the Organization of Petroleum Exporting Countries (OPEC) and cashed in on the rising international price of oil. But, we have seen that by the early 1980s, when Nigeria had returned to civilian rule, world oil prices declined, leading to economic problems due to the country's almost total dependence on oil revenues.

As oil income began to rebound in the 1990s, the local delta people began to find themselves in a losing battle with the oil companies and the central government. The national administration siphoned off most of the income from the oil production, leaving little for the development of the delta area or for the protection of the fragile fishing and agricultural environment there. These problems have continued to the present day. Oil flares from the burning off excess byproducts from oil production light up the sky. Oil spills damage both fishing and farming for the local people. Noise and air pollution degrade the quality of life. Huge explosions, often caused by people cutting into oil pipelines to steal gasoline, have caused hundreds of deaths. A correspondent who has studied the area reports, "The immense wealth oil represented was there to see but not to touch. People felt abandoned by the newly independent government and the companies that removed petroleum from their land but provided scarce educational and health facilities in return."[3]

The protests of one of the smallest ethnic groups in the area brought these problems to international attention. The writer and television producer Ken Saro-Wiwa organized his people, the Ogoni, and helped to found a protest group, the Movement for the Salvation of the Ogoni People, or MOSOP. Saro-Wiwa and his supporters led protests throughout Ogoniland and led tours of devastated farmlands and villages for visiting journalists and environmentalists. When Abacha replaced Babangida as head of the government, crackdowns by the security forces became even more destructive. A split developed between more conservative Ogoni chiefs and elders and the youth movement of Saro-Wiwa. In May of 1994, members of the youth movement attacked and killed some of these elders and chiefs, leading the government's arrest and execution of Saro-Wiwa after a swift military hearing, which did not allow the defendants normal due process. Saro-Wiwa's son, Ken Wiwa, has continued to focus international attention on the plight of his people and environmental damage in the delta.

The much larger Ijaw community has continued and escalated the local people's resistance to the government and oil companies. The Ijaw represent a set of linguistically related populations who in modern times have come to think of themselves as a unified ethnic group of nearly 14 million (by way of comparison, the Ogoni population is approximately 300,000). They are now the largest group in the region of the Niger Delta. Along with the neighboring Itsekiri, they were historically among some of the first people to encounter and trade with the Europeans along the coast. Since the late 1990s, the Ijaw and Itsekiri have come to violent conflict over the distribution of political representation in the larger delta region, related to hopes for access to governmental funds for development.

Violence has also been sparked by government mobile security forces, nicknamed the "Kill-and-Go," occasionally called in by oil companies for protection. These clashes escalated in 1999, leading to the infamous "Odi Massacre" in November of that year, in which the entire Ijaw village of Odi was destroyed by security forces. Groups within the Ijaw community have responded with the formation of militant organizations, some fomenting attacks on oil and government installations, some calling for outright independence of the Niger Delta region. After the re-election of Obasanjo in 2003, the most visible of these groups has been the Movement for Emancipation of the Niger Delta, or MEND. In April of 2006, attacks attributed to MEND reduced oil production by as much as 25 percent.[4]

In summary, for hundreds of years resources have been extracted from the Niger Delta: first palm oil and slaves and now petroleum. Vast revenues from oil exports have benefited national politicians and central government but have not provided real benefits or economic development for the local Nigerian communities, who consequently feel exploited. Increasing violence in the region has been the result, as local protesters demand compensation for environmental and economic degradation of their homelands. The violence involves not only attacks on oil installations (mainly kidnapping or taking hostages of oil workers) and clashes with the military, but also some interethnic clashes as well.

Communal Conflict and Nigeria

A recurring theme in the history of modern Nigeria is regional, ethnic, and religious conflict. We have seen that such conflicts have been exacerbated by features of the colonial and independent state. Competition for power and access to resources became much more serious under these systems. Groups that had not even thought of themselves as unified or identifiable communities coalesced as such competition intensified. The emergence of an Ijaw identity discussed in the previous section illustrates this process. Still, as Nigeria enters the twenty-first century, the most dangerous line of division may be that of religion.

Islam came to the Hausa states and Kanem-Bornu in the north between 600 and 800 years ago. Hausa traditions, we have seen, reflect a strongly Muslim culture. At the beginning of the nineteenth century, the jihads of the Fulani, under Uthman dan Fodio, united much of the north in the Hausa-Fulani empire of Sokoto. Christian conversions in the south go back to the early explorations of the Portuguese, who brought Catholicism to Benin as well as coastal areas. This early contact was thin, but Christian missionaries became very active in the nineteenth century, during the British anti-slavery campaign. In the colonial era, the country was divided between the Muslim north and the Christian south.

This religious divide remains a dangerous trigger for internal conflict. For example, in 1986 Babangida, after coming to power, attempted to make Nigeria a full member of Organization of Islamic Countries, touching off protests and riots in northern cities, including Kano and Kaduna. Another example began with an attempt by a Christian fundamentalist evangelist to hold a revival in Kano in 1991. Hausa youths (no doubt some of them "area boys," as young toughs are called in Nigeria), attacked districts housing Igbo traders, erected burning barricades, and at least for a day overwhelmed the local police and security forces. Some of the militants' anger possibly derived from the government's refusal to allow Louis Farrakhan of the American Nation of Islam to speak in Kano.[5]

After the restoration of civilian government in 1998, and the election of President Obasanjo, northern Muslims began to campaign for local institution of Shari'a law in local and state jurisdictions. The civilian constitution now in place did allow for local option for customary and Shari's courts, particularly for domestic or family cases. Whether customary courts, specifically those implementing Shari's, could also judge criminal cases is less clear, but that is what many northerners now demanded. The non-Muslim minority in northern states feared they would be subject to the harsh judicial code of Shari'a, allowing for amputations for theft, stoning for adultery, and whipping and caning for other offenses. The issue came to head in October of 1999 when the governor of the far northern state of Zamfara announced the state would institute Shari'a as the legal system of the state in January of 2000.

Violence broke out in several northern and Middle-Belt cities when other state governments announced the implementation of Shari'a in 2000. Over 1,000 people were estimated to have been killed in Kaduna, for instance, from February to May of that year. Fighting also broke out in several locations in the Middle-Belt region. This area around the confluence of the Niger and Benue Rivers has become a flash-point for communal conflict. It marks a boundary area, between the predominantly Muslim territory to the north, and the mostly Christian areas to the south. Local peoples in this intermediate area have long felt threatened and oppressed by incursions of the Hausa-Fulani as a consequence of the jihad begun by Uthman dan Fodio in the 1800s. Violent outbreaks took hundreds or thousands of lives in the area around the city of Jos from 2001 through 2004. President Obasanjo has wavered on just how to deal with unrest associated with the imposition of Shari'a law. His vacillation could be one of the main explanations for the lack of northern electoral support he received in the elections of 2003 (when, as we have seen, a northerner, Mohammed Buhari, swept the polls in the north).

One very prominent case brought the tension over Shari's to international attention. In 2002 a woman in the northern state of Katsina was convicted of adultery and sentenced to be executed by stoning. The Muslim court based its decision on the fact that the woman had a baby while not married (she was divorced at the time). Normally, four eye-witnesses are required to prove such a case, but not so when the mother is unmarried. The issue is more complicated than it might appear, because different schools of Islamic law provide differing interpretations on when and under what conditions the circumstantial evidence of pregnancy is sufficient for conviction. There was an international storm of protest, in the United States reaching even to the television show of Oprah Winfrey, calling for petitions to the Nigerian government. Appeals and other hearings on the case were postponed until after the presidential elections in Nigeria of 2003. A higher

Shari'a court of appeal in Katsina state ultimately overturned the conviction and the woman was not stoned to death. This case, however, did serve to bring the Shari's controversy in Nigeria to international attention.

The religious dividing line in Nigeria, with the Muslim north and the Christian south, continues to be a major fault line threatening the peace and unity of the nation. People of both faiths are often thrown together in large cities, such as Lagos, Kano, and Kaduna, leading to greater chance of friction and outbreaks of violence. Also, the smaller ethnic groups in the Middle Belt often feel themselves under attack from the dominant Hausa-Fulani, whose Muslim faith adds a religious current to the tension.

Conclusions

Can Nigeria become a successful and strong state, overcoming the centrifugal forces outlined in this last chapter? There are reasons for hope. Nigeria is certainly better off than many new nations in sub-Saharan Africa in terms of its economic and educational foundations. The cultural heritage of the country can be an additional source of strength. Some of the most prominent universities in the continent are in Nigeria, including the Universities of Ibadan, of Nsukka, and Muhammad Bello University. Nigeria has one of the most outstanding artistic traditions of any state in Africa. Several Nigerian authors have become international literary figures: Wole Soyinka, Nigeria's winner of the Nobel Prize for Literature; Chinua Achebe, famous for the prototypical novels of African's experience with colonialism; Ben Okri, Amos Tutuola, Buchi Emecheta, Zaynab Alkali, and poets like John Pepper Clark, and playwrights such as Femi Osofisan; the list could go on and on.

The major challenges facing the country have been outlined over the last several chapters: an economy based on extraction of natural resources and too dependent on a single commodity; a weak political culture at the national level; the reinforcing divisions of regionalism, ethnic rivalry, and religion. Many of these challenges lead to a lack of national unity and can be summed up by a passage near the end of Achebe's fourth novel, about modern African politics, *A Man of the People*. A corrupt politician has been brought down because of his excesses. The Igbo said of him that he had "taken enough for the owner to see." The protagonist meditates on these words, that same he had heard when villagers punished a petty thief years before. "The owner of the village and the village had a mind; it could say no to sacrilege," he thinks. "But in the affairs of the nation there was no owner, the laws of the village became powerless."[6] Achebe's narrator implies that new political traditions must be forged to create a national sense of ownership. Soyinka's play, *Death and the King's Horseman*, tells of the tragedy of a great man, who had been granted honor and riches as the holder of the important ceremonial position of horseman to the King of Oyo. His tragic fall was occasioned by his becoming an "eater of leftovers," that is, a great man who does not leave enough of his wealth and honor for others but takes all for himself (does not even leave leftovers on his plate for others). Too often, Soyinka implies, national leaders in Nigeria have taken all for themselves, leaving not even leftovers for the common people, as in the oil-rich Niger Delta.

Africans have been adaptable throughout history—traditions have changed; change has resulted in new traditions. Nigeria may have the power and resources to be the leader among African states in carrying on this process of change and tradition.

References

1. These machinations are set forth in an autobiography by Wole Soyinka (2006). *You Must Set Forth at Dawn: A Memoir*. New York: Random House, pp. 120–140.

2. William D. Graf (1988). *The Nigerian State: Political Economy, State Class and Political System in the Post-Colonial Era*. London: Heinemann Educational Books, p. 95.

3. Karl Maier (2000). *This House Has Fallen: Midnight in Nigeria*. New York: Public Affairs, p. 85.

4. BBC News, website, April 20, 2006, accessed at http://news.bbc.co.uk/2/hi/africa/4732210.stm.

5. Maier, p. 164.

6. Chinua Achebe (1967). *A Man of the People*. Garden City, New Jersey: Anchor Press, p. 140–141.

Index